Running out of space — What are the alternatives?

GLORIA NOVAK

EDITOR
Library Space Planner,
University of California at Berkeley

PROCEEDINGS OF THE PRECONFERENCE, JUNE 1975, SAN FRANCISCO
Sponsored by the BUILDINGS FOR COLLEGE AND UNIVERSITY
LIBRARIES COMMITTEE, BUILDINGS AND EQUIPMENT SECTION of the
LIBRARY ADMINISTRATION DIVISION,

AMERICAN LIBRARY ASSOCIATION, Chicago 1978

Library of Congress Cataloging in Publication Data

Main entry under title:

Running out of space--what are the alternatives?

   1. Libraries--Space utilization--Congresses.
2. Books--Storage--Congresses. I. Novak, Gloria.
II. American Library Association. Buildings for
College and University Libraries Committee.
Z679.55.R85   022   78-1796
ISBN 0-8389-3215-0

Printed in the United States of America

Running out of space—
What are
the alternatives?

Contents

Preface

The objective of the preconference was to address a library problem
which seems to defy solution - running out of space. The preconference
was planned for librarians, administrators of educational institutions,
library trustees, state and institutional budget officers, all those associated with library facilities currently experiencing serious space
problems or which are expected to face these problems in the near future.

Libraries are faced with tight budgets, whatever the source of support. They are faced with ecological considerations - from limitation of
land use, to energy conservation, to retrofitting existing buildings rather than constructing new ones. The economy is unpredictable, and ecological considerations are too often inadequately understood and misapplied.

Members of the Building Committee for College and University Libraries had long discussed the possibility of sponsoring a preconference on
book storage at the San Francisco American Library Association conference.
By the time specific plans were formulated, however, the members had begun to view book storage as only part of the much larger problem of running out of space. Book storage represents merely one alternative to
solving this problem. Others needed to be explored. Microform collections, new types of equipment, increased sharing of resources through regional cooperation, and new construction were other alternatives the committee envisioned as potential solutions. Speakers were selected to discuss each alternative, and they were asked to consider the implications
that implementation of their alternative would have for space requirements,
costs, public service, and staff. New construction was deliberately list-
ed last because each member recognized that an existing library building
is often so totally inadequate for the service it must provide that it can
not be made to work effectively, no matter how imaginative a librarian's
approach to an alternative may be. This solution raises the most serious
obstacle to resolving the space problem - lack of funds. Librarians have
struggled with this problem for a long time, successfully in the 1960s.

With the inflation-recession syndrome of the 1970s and with the changing
social climate, old methods of justifying requests for financing new construction were severely scrutinized and new questions raised and old answers rejected. An individual involved in this question-raising process
was added to the program to help librarians gain a new, or at least a different, perspective on the economic realities and to provide clues for librarians to develop new strategies and effective justifications for requests
for construction funds.

The rate of change in the field of information continues to pick up
momentum. Libraries are old and traditional institutions and, for a variety of reasons, find it difficult to respond in a timely fashion to many
of these changes. Looking toward the possible discovery of yet another
alternative to that ubiquitous space problem, the invitation went to a
person outside the library world, skilled in problem-solving and active in
the forefront of the forces of change, who would be willing to share with
librarians his perception of today's library and what it must do to meet
tomorrow's challenge.

The committee recognized that each alternative raised a series of complex problems of its own and that the preconference time which could be
allotted to each was too limited to fully address all of them. However,
it was primarily their intent to indicate that there are alternatives to
solving library space problems, to indicate that no alternative is a panacea, and hopefully to reveal the most significant benefits and the most
serious shortcomings of each alternative. Recognizing also that most of
these alternatives are by no means new, the committee hoped that the program as formatted might provide the audience with fresh viewpoints and
new insights into the problems they face.

Acknowledgments

The success of the preconference was due to the efforts and remarkable teamwork of a large group of American Library Association
members. I would like to give special thanks to the good-natured and
supportive members of the Building Committee for College and University Libraries:

JAMES B. ALSIP   Moderator, *New Building, Library Addition
or Renovation?*
Assistant Director for Technical Services
University of Oklahoma

RAYMOND A. BOHLING Director of Publicity
Assistant Director for Administration
University of Minnesota

BERNARD KREISSMAN Moderator, *Regional Cooperation,
An Alternative to Running Out of Space?*
University Librarian
University of California at Davis

NANCY R. McADAMS   Audio/visual Director and Speaker
Library Facilities Planner
University of Texas at Austin

FRAZER G. POOLE   Speaker
Assistant Director for Preservation
Library of Congress

LEON RANEY   Arrangements
Director of Libraries
South Dakota State University

JOHN VASI   Moderator, *Are Microforms an Answer/Partial
                       Answer to Library Space Problems?*
                       Assistant to the Director for Facilities Planning
                       State University of New York at Buffalo

ROBERT R. WALSH   Speaker
                       Assistant University Librarian for Building Planning
                       Harvard University

       I would also like to thank

DAVID R. SMITH   Coordinator, *Equipment Affecting Space Utilization*
                       Director, Public Service Division
                       Hennepin County, Minnesota
                       Chairman, Equipment Committee

JERROLD ORNE   Moderator, *Equipment Affecting Space Utilization*
                       Professor, School of Library Science
                       University of North Carolina

                                      Gloria Novak, Chair
                                      Building Committee for
                                      College and University Libraries

Book storage

INTRODUCTION

Book storage is an old issue for libraries, yet in the 1970s it is as controversial as it has ever been. With Harvard University Library as one of the pioneers in developing off-campus book storage, their decision to construct a building addition for the central collections on campus - an old crowded campus - was provocative. It is apparent that book storage for Harvard is only one of a number of simultaneously utilized alternatives for resolving the problem of running out of space.

It is interesting to note that when the University of Washington's proposed library storage facility was initially included in the preconference program, construction was imminent. By the time the program presentation was made, the governor of that state had halted the project and requested a study to determine "the feasibility and alternatives to a library materials central storage facility for both public and academic libraries." Not only are the early issues of book storage still with us and unresolved, but state funding authorities are now playing an active role in the decision to store or not to store.

More and more libraries are turning to storage as an answer to their space problems.* There are problems and pitfalls. However, new technology may help to cope with some of these and provide new methods of approach to this alternative.

*George Piternick, *Book Storage in Academic Libraries,* a report submitted to The Council on Library Resources, (Vancouver, Canada: 1974).

Harvard University's storage experience

ROBERT R. WALSH

Assistant University Librarian for Building Planning
Harvard University Library

Almost thirty years ago, Joseph Hudnut, who was then the Dean of the Harvard Graduate School of Design, wrote of the dramatic and threatening rate of growth of the Harvard University Library. He predicted a great mound of books, as high as the pyramids, covering the famous Harvard Yard. He also noted the pattern of the development of departmental and special libraries at Harvard, stating that the library "does not grow like a melon, enlarging its periphery in concentric rings, but like a strawberry plant which sends out creepers which take root and blossom into baby libraries." He then stated:

> The (Harvard) Library holds 5,600,000 books and doubles in size every fifteen years. In 1962 it will have 11,000,000 books; in 1977, 22,000,000; and in 2060, 1,400,000,000. By that time it will have extended to the edges of the Harvard Yard, having thrown all other buildings over the fence into Harvard Square. The space now occupied by Philosophy Hall will be devoted to 30,000 items on the literature of the Congo; University Hall will be sunk under 400,000 (volumes) on Oceania; and the Appleton Chapel...will be remembered as the site afterwards consecrated to 500,000 incunabula on *Imitatio Christi*.

Hudnut's dire prediction has not exactly come true. Today the Harvard library system is just under 10 million volumes. But with almost 100 separate library units comprising the system, the Harvard University Library, perhaps more than any other library, has firsthand experience with almost every conceivable form of physical facility. There are the libraries of the Graduate schools, such as the Baker Library of the Graduate School of Business Administration. There are libraries based on language, such as the Harvard-Yenching Library for East Asian materials.

3

There are departmental subject libraries, such as those in history and chemistry. There are undergraduate libraries, such as Lamont and Hilles. There are libraries based on form, such as the Houghton Library for rare books and manuscripts, and the Government Department Data Center, consisting largely of magnetic tapes. There are area center libraries, interdisciplinary libraries, and house libraries in the undergraduate residential houses. And there are some highly specialized and arcane libraries, such as the Farlow Library of Cryptogamic Botany, the Oakes Ames Orchid Library, and the Milman Parry Collection of Oral Literature. Indeed, if one wanted to be cynical, one would not liken it to a strawberry plant as did Hudnut, but to a weed patch gone wild.

It is not my intention here to describe or defend the existence of the myriad number of libraries which comprise the system, other than to point out that most of the libraries grew out of a response to certain needs in one or another area of the University; and also to point out that the exact number of libraries changes from one year to another, as libraries are created or done away with, usually absorbed by a larger unit in the system. What I do intend to describe is the pattern of storage of material that was developed in the system to house the collections.

When the Harry Elkins Widener Library opened in 1915, it was thought that this spacious building, with a capacity for almost 3 million volumes, would satisfy the space needs for the central research collections in Humanities and the social sciences for the Faculty of Arts and Sciences for the rest of the twentieth century. In fact, two of its ten levels of self-supporting bookstacks were left unshelved, as it was thought that this shelving would not be needed for many years to come. However, when Keyes Metcalf came to Harvard in 1937 as Director of the University Library and Librarian of Harvard College, Widener, though only twenty two years old, was nearly full. The Library for the Graduate School of Business Administration had already moved out of Widener into its own building in 1926. In his annual report for 1939/40, Metcalf called for a solution to this space problem. I might point out here that the concern was not only crowding of the collection, but also the need for more staff and reader space; however, our concern in these discussions is with the housing of the collections. Metcalf spelled out a four-point plan which would be an alternate to building yet another massive research library. He called for the construction of new, special facilities. These included a rare books library, an undergraduate library, underground stacks beneath the Harvard Yard contiguous to Widener, and an out-of-house facility for the storing of less used material still deemed to have research value. In 1942, after several years of negotiating for incorporation as a separate corporation, the New England Deposit Library was opened. This was not strictly a Harvard facility, but a separate institution whose membership included several Boston area university and research libraries including Harvard. It was the first successful attempt at interinstitutional storage of less used materials.

Spatially, the NEDL is a compact boxy warehouse with two parts. The front part contains a reading room, work areas, and mechanical space. The larger rear part is an oblong box measuring 64 by 88 feet, and contains six levels of stack. It is a highly efficient bookstack, with one center aisle and all narrow stack aisles dead-ending at the outside walls. The shelving is either wood or metal bolted together, and although this makes for less flexibility, most depositors elected to shelve their material by size, increasing the compactness of the storage: in some areas we get as many as 10 shelves per section. It is estimated that the NEDL can contain approximately one million volumes, at an average of 30 volumes per square foot.

Also in 1942, Harvard opened the second element in the Metcalf proposal - the Houghton Library for rare books and manuscripts. This building of 38,000 sq.ft. was provided with an air-conditioning system to maintain optimum temperature and humidity for preservation, a special new kind of cool lighting, and stack shelving designed to minimize the danger of damage to bindings. Houghton allowed for the removal of the special collections department from Widener, and for the systematic transfer of rare material from the Widener stack, allowing growth within that stack for the research collection. This pattern of transfer of material from the Widener stack, allowing for more growth within it, has occurred with frequency and regularity.

In 1949, the third and fourth elements of the Metcalf plan came into being. The Lamont Library was opened. Beneath the Lamont Library proper were constructed two levels of bookstack, one for expansion of the Widener stack and connected to it by tunnel, and one for the expansion of the Houghton stack and connected to it. This was the first phase of stack storage beneath the Harvard Yard. The Lamont Library proper was the first separate undergraduate library in a university, and provided completely open stacks and a wide variety of accommodations for readers. Lamont did not specifically make more room in the Widener stack, but it did relieve the Widener reading rooms from the pressure of undergraduate use.

Metcalf concluded that section of his annual report for 1939/40 which described this four-point plan by stating: "When these four units are provided, there will be available sufficient book shelving for at least thirty years." This, alas, would not be the case. As Widener began to fill up again, more transfers occurred, often planned in conjunction with new construction expanding a subject or departmental library. The construction of an addition to the Music Department in 1956 allowed for the transfer of research materials in this subject out of Widener. The Music Library was further expanded with yet another addition in 1972, which allowed for further consolidation as it made space to incorporate the Isham Memorial Library of early instrumental and vocal music, a collection largely in microform and previously housed in Memorial Church. I point this out because we often see at Harvard, contrary to popular myth, the consolidation and contraction of collections, and not just ever-expanding numbers.

In 1963, the construction of an addition to the Fogg Museum of Art allowed for the transfer of the research collection in fine arts from Widener to the Fogg, where it was merged with the smaller working library of the Museum. Again, in 1972, the construction of Monroe C. Gutman Library of the Graduate School of Education, with 87,000 sq.ft. of library space, allowed us to transfer out of Widener some 60,000 volumes on education and the history of education. The Gutman Library also absorbed a superb historical collection of secondary-school textbooks which were stored in the NEDL. And with the opening of the new Undergraduate Science Center in 1973, the new Godfrey Lowell Cabot Science Library came into being. Primarily an undergraduate library for the sciences, it nonetheless incorporated the research collections in mathematics and statistics, removing them from Widener, and allowing once again for breathing space in the central collection. Similarly, it is expected that the several departmental science libraries, located in the research laboratories, will periodically transfer older retrospective material in the several scientific disciplines to the Cabot Library, keeping only the current research material in house. This, it is hoped, will have some effect in keeping a lid on the physical growth of the science libraries, and also eliminate some duplication, especially in retrospective holdings of serials. As these transfers occur over the years, it is envisaged that the bulk of the historical material in science will be found in Cabot, and we can then transfer the history of science materials there from Widener.

By now you must think that everything conceivable had been taken out of Widener and put somewhere else. But alas, life being what it is, that is not the case. Even anticipating all of the recent transfers I have just described, a Ten Year Planning Study prepared in 1966 stated that:

> Widener, with its stack level beneath Lamont, now provides approximately 318,000 square feet. We believe that plans should be made as soon as possible for an additional 200,000.

The Planning Study went on to state:

> At the present time Widener houses the basic research collections of the University in the humanities, history, and the social sciences. In approximate terms one can say that, aside from general works and a few collections too small to affect calculations for this purpose, one-third of the Widener collections is classified as History, one-third in the Economics, Government, and Sociology classes that are very closely related to History, and nearly one-third as Language and Literature.

> Pressure for space during recent years has largely dictated decisions on deployment of the collections; any proposal for removing a subject from Widener has seemed almost irresistibly attractive, and any suggestion for extending the scope of its research fields has seemed almost unthinkable.

> If the central collections as now constituted are to be kept together, and their interrelationships are such as to reinforce the case for close proximity, the most desirable arrangement for the future would

appear to be a large annex to Widener, connected
with it if possible by both underground stacks and
bridges.

After numerous site studies and feasibility studies, and after a
long fund-raising campaign, what was called for in the Ten Year Planning
Study began to take form as the Nathan Marsh Pusey Library, the second
phase of library construction beneath the Harvard Yard. Originally
thought of as a totally below-grade building, careful and imaginative
planning on the part of the architects, Hugh Stubbins and Associates of
Cambridge, has allowed us to exploit the attributes of the site in order
to bring light and a sense of outlook into the staff and reader spaces
of the Pusey Library.

The site consisted of a small hill, with a grade differential of ten
feet from one end to the other. We were able to pick up this hill, flat-
ten it out, and tuck the library underneath it. Then by means of a perimeter moat, masked by a grassy berm, we can introduce light and a
sense of outlook to the staff and reader areas of the top level of what
is essentially a three-story below-grade library. In addition, near the
center of the building is a 50 foot by 50 foot light court, fully landscaped, which extends to the first and second levels, bringing additional
outlook to the interior of the library.

With its 87,000 sq.ft. the Pusey Library will allow for the growth
of the collections in Widener and Houghton for the next fifteen to twenty
years. It is also designed so that an additional amount of library space,
up to a maximum of another 160,000 sq.ft., can be built in subsequent
phases of below-ground and above-ground construction, part of which assumes that an adjacent building, the former Presidents' House, will be
relocated or demolished. We have planned the library so that if it is
necessary, and if funds are available, we can continue underground construction from the present foundation of Pusey to the street, with the
possibility of up to four stories of above-ground construction on top
of the building.

The Pusey Library, like other examples cited, makes room in Widener
and Houghton proper by removing fairly self-sufficient elements. It also
has a general stack area which connects with the lowest level of the
Widener stack and will accommodate further growth in the stack. The
other four elements which will be relocated in the Pusey Library are the
University Archives, including its stack, staff, and reader areas; the
Harvard Theatre Collection of the Houghton Library, also with its stack,
staff, and reader areas; the Map Collection again with its staff, reader
areas, and map cases. Each one of these is a fairly independent unit,
in bibliographic terms, of the library and was seen as capable of being
located in an annex. The Pusey Library will also have a stack area to
house the manuscript collection of the Houghton Library. There is one
other important aspect of the Pusey Library. Throughout the design,
the client and the architects worked hard to achieve the desire that it
be a linking building, and that Pusey itself, and any further additional
construction, continue the physical integration of the library complex
in this corner of the Harvard Yard. The design is such that one can
move freely from one element of the complex to another, once admitted

to the bookstack, with the exception, of course, of the areas housing the rare or restricted collections. As the Librarian of the Houghton Library has put it, "Pusey must make the whole more than the sum of its parts."

Land use was certainly uppermost in our thinking of constructing a largely underground building, especially on a site as well known and historical as the Harvard Yard. The building was designed before the "energy crisis" occurred, but we find by happy accident we have a highly insulated building. It is largely below ground, with the soil temperature changing less radically throughout the year than the air temperature. For security reasons we have triple-glazed windows, again excellent insulation. The roof is landscaped and covered with three to five feet of earth. Thus we find we have a highly efficient building in terms of energy use.

All that I have been describing has had to do mainly with the central collections of the Harvard College Library, which is the library of the Faculty of Arts and Sciences, and with its effects on other departmental libraries. But rest assured that other elements of the University Library system were not lying dormant; they, too, were growing, and many experiencing periodic space crunches. A wide variety of methods has been used to alleviate this. The library for the Law School seized the opportunity in 1950 to carve out some storage for itself. At that time a large graduate housing complex was being designed by Walter Gropius just north of the Law School, and the Law Library was able to lay hold of 8,000 sq.ft. of basement areas in these dormitories, where they erected their own kind of compact shelving, with stack sections eight to ten shelves high, and very narrow 20-inch aisles. Like the Widener books in NEDL, these are for the storage of little used material. In 1959 a building was built for International Legal Studies, and the material on international law was moved out of the Law Library and into its own 16,000-sq.ft. library.

At the Divinity School a new library was built for the Andover-Harvard Theological Library in 1961, but built contiguous to the old self-supporting stack in Divinity Hall so that it might still be used by the library. Furthermore, the new library was built in such a way that an additional two floors can be built on top of the new structure in the future. Finally, at the Andover-Harvard Library a decision was reached a few years ago to shift from a local classification system to LC, and a decision was made at the same time not to re-classify the existing collection. This meant that the books in the older classification scheme could be compacted on the shelves, since there was no need for growth, and this allowed for all those linear feet of shelving to be available for new acquisitions.

Other tricks have been played. At the Cabot Library, mentioned earlier, we found that the main stack level, in the basement, was to have a slab-to-slab distance of over twelve feet, due to the location of large mechanical spaces with this height requirement elsewhere on the same floor. Borrowing an idea we saw at the Rockefeller Library at Brown University, we fully stacked this area the entire height of twelve feet, therefore gaining four shelves of storage above the usual seven, and creating an in-house deposit situation. Also in the Pusey Library we had the cubage to install shelving 100 inches tall, gaining an eighth shelf throughout, and an additional 14 per cent capacity in the same floor space. At the Gutman Library, the top floor of the building houses faculty offices, and is at the moment functionally separate from the library. However, if it is deemed necessary in the future, the library could take over this floor, which is constructed identically to the two stack levels beneath it, and gain an additional 18,000 sq.ft.

To pick up Hudnut's metaphor on the strawberry plant once again, I must point out here that not all strawberries survive; some die and some are eaten. In time, many small special libraries, which grew up to meet the needs of a special program, are absorbed into larger units when the need for the special program diminishes. Sometimes a library will shrink. The new facility for the Littauer Library of economics and government, which is being planned in conjunction with the John Fitzgerald Kennedy School of Government, may actually be smaller than the space it presently occupies because much of the federal and state document material housed in Littauer is now available in microform, and we can dispose of the hard copy. Also, our membership in the Center for Research Libraries for the past ten years is seen as having some effect on growth, as will our participation in the Research Libraries Group.

Planning for a storage facility at the University of Washington libraries

MARGARET B. TJADEN
Planning Assistant, University of Washington Libraries

The University of Washington's alternative for resolving its library space problems is a new book storage facility to be constructed on the campus. This narrative will begin with the historical pattern of this institution's library space problems and their solutions, which in turn created the context for the current space problem and its proposed solution. This historical description will be followed by some discussion of the draft building program developed by the Ad Hoc Programming Committee, the benefits of this alternative, and the current status of the proposed solution.

HISTORY

1927   Construction was completed on the central library building designed for a capacity of 200,000 volumes.

1931   Only four years later, the building was seriously overcrowded.

1935   An addition was built to house a growing staff and the School of Librarianship. This addition did little to alleviate the space problem for the collection, which had grown to 294,000 volumes, and storage outside the central library building began.

1945   Development of branch libraries gained momentum. However, the facilities selected did not provide space for long-term growth of the collections nor for an increase in the user population. When space began to run out in a branch, books were either stored in closets or in similar space in the building in which the branch was located or transferred to the central library.

1948   A 300,000-volume, modular bookstack addition to the central li-
        brary was completed. It had been expected that with this addi-
        tional capacity, all stored materials would be returned to the
        central library. However, this was not possible, and on-campus
        storage in any space available continued.

1956   A ten-year plan was developed which proposed construction of two
        additions to the central library over the 1957-61 period, an un-
        dergraduate library in 1961-63 and an underground storage facil-
        ity in 1963-65.

1963   An addition to the central library was completed, bringing its
        total capacity to 1,200,000 volumes. The sub-basement was
        planned specifically for storage and staging, with a capacity
        of 210,000 volumes; this plan was later compromised when it be-
        came necessary to use a portion of the area to house a part of
        the acquisition division's staff. By 1963, the number of branch
        libraries had increased to eighteen; the total campus collection
        consisted of 1,250,000 volumes; and the campus population con-
        sisted of 21,000 students.

1965-72 For the first time the library administration placed a separate
        storage facility on its capital budget request for the 1967-69
        biennium. It failed to be included in the University's budget
        request to the Governor for that biennium. Although the li-
        brary administration continued to include a storage facility in
        its capital budget request each biennium thereafter, the univer-
        sity administration was not convinced of the need for it. How-
        ever, they did agree to requests for the construction of an un-
        dergraduate library and new facilities for, or expansion of,
        over half of the existing branch libraries.

1973   By the summer of 1973 almost every unit in the library system
        was being adversely affected by the lack of bookstack space.
        Seats were being traded for bookstacks, and the public access
        collection in the central library was more and more taking on
        the look of a storage collection.

        The library administration realized that they had to present
        their need for a storage facility in a more compelling fashion
        if a crisis situation was to be avoided. During that summer
        they developed an extensive, comprehensive, quantitative state-
        ment on the space problem and the impact, in terms of loss of
        user seats and curtailment of some collecting programs, if no
        action were taken to alleviate it.

        For the first time, the impact statement also recommended that
        the expansion needs of the University Records Center be met in
        the proposed storage facility. The Records Center is adminis-
        tered by the library, and its space problems had been of concern
        to the University administration for some time. The University

was persuaded of the need for a storage facility and in 1974
placed it on its 1975-77 Capital Construction request list.

PLANNING THE STORAGE FACILITY

An Ad Hoc Programming Committee was formed consisting of staff librarians, the manager of the University Records Center, and a campus architect. The charge to the committee was to develop a draft building
program for submittal to the Board of Regents. The following are various
aspects of the building program that were considered by the committee and
some of the factors which determined program requirements.

Site

The site-selection factor considered most important by the committee
was close proximity to the campus and, in particular, to the central library and the existing University Records Center. This strong preference
was based in part on the experience with the temporary book-shelving arrangements made during the construction of the 1963 addition to the central library. At that time a large portion of the collection was moved
to the basement of a dormitory located seven minutes walking distance
from the central library. Library patrons were extremely reluctant to
walk that distance to obtain library materials. Experiences at other institutions corroborated the committee's opinion that close proximity to
the central campus area is an essential element in the success of a book
storage facility.

The University gave the Libraries two options for siting on currently
owned land. Only one satisfied the requirement that it be near both the
central library and the University Records Center. This site is a fifteen-minute walk from the library and a seven-minute walk from the Center.
The University has reserved this preferred parcel of land for the storage
facility.

Building Type

The building is planned for temperature and humidity control and will
have no windows, except in the office areas. A one-story building would
reduce building costs by eliminating the need for both elevators and the
additional structural strength required for multi-storied buildings; however, because of the limitation of site size, a three-story building is
required to fulfill the total storage space requirements.

Building Size

The committee recommended a 100,000 assignable sq.ft. storage facility
to be constructed in two increments of equal size. The first 50,000 assignable sq.ft. increment was programmed to house the following elements:

1. *Bookstack Area* - The size of this area was based on the need to

store 631,000 volumes, which, at a capacity of 20 volumes per sq.ft., would require a total of 31,550 sq.ft. If this project were approved for funding in 1975-77, the bookstacks would have been filled to capacity by July, 1980.

2. *Public Service Area* - This area will consist of a reading room where patrons may consult materials which will be brought from the stacks in any amount for their convenience and a facility for charging out materials.

3. *Staff Work Area* - This area must support the activities of two full-time classified staff members and the equivalent of one full-time student who will work primarily in the bookstack area and must also provide space for a staff-mediated photo-copy machine.

4. *University Records Center* - This area will provide additional storage, staff, and user space for the Center and will be secure from the book storage portion of the building.

To minimize cost, common restrooms, staff lounge, and loading dock facilities are planned to serve the book storage and University Records Center functions.

Shelving

The 31,550 sq.ft. space requirement for the bookstack area is based on the assumption that the books will be shelved in call number order and that standard library shelving will be utilized. However, the ultimate decision as to the type of shelving to be utilized will depend upon the resolution of the conflict between the user's desire to be able to browse the stored collection and the library's need for efficient use of the storage space. Electrically operated compact shelving would substantial-ly increase the volume capacity of the proposed storage facility, an in-crease of such a dimension that the need for the second building increment could be postponed for at least fifteen years beyond the 1980 date pro-jected on the basis of the use of standard shelving.

BIBLIOGRAPHICAL AND PHYSICAL ACCESS
TO STORED MATERIALS

The proposed procedures for access to materials in storage emphasize ease of access for the user to encourage maximum use of the stored collec-tion. The following are some tentative proposals not yet worked out in detail.

Transportation and Delivery Service

A transportation service to the facility is required to minimize the bar-rier that even a fifteen-minute walk from the central library might create.

Pickup and delivery of stored materials is to be made on a regular, twice-a-day schedule with delivery to the requesting library unit based on 24-hour service.

Bibliographical Access to Materials in Storage

Public records will be altered to indicate the storage location.
A single-entry file of the storage facility holdings will be created and
located in the facility.
A circulation file will be maintained in the storage facility.

The user's bibliographical approach to materials located in the
storage facility will be through the public catalogs located in the central and branch libraries and/or through the holdings file at the facility itself. The user can elect either to have the materials paged and
delivered to a specific library unit or to go directly to the storage facility and use or check out the materials there. If the user does not
have the proper entry for locating the material in the facility's file,
a staff member will call the central library for assistance in identifying the entry.

COSTS

There is a variety of costs to be taken into account as the planning for the storage facility proceeds. Some are in the category of
one-time costs and others are added operational cost.

One-Time Costs

Building and equipment costs for the proposed first increment of the University of Washington's storage facility based on 60,000 gross
sq.ft. and on the use of standard shelving is $2,800,000. This
includes miscellaneous costs such as fees, sales tax, and other
equipment required to complete the project. If electric compact
shelving is used in place of standard shelving, the cost will be
increased dramatically. In addition, compact shelving would increase construction costs, because of the resultant need to double the floor load capacity of the building.
Initial moving to storage of approximately 217,000 volumes, including selection, changing of records, and creation of a new file, is envisioned as being executed as a single project. The cost for
this project has not yet been estimated.

Added Operational Costs

Transportation and delivery service.
Additional staff for the facility - three full-time equivalents.
Continuing program of transferring materials to storage.

Since definitive, final planning for the physical facility and its
operation has not yet been done, cost information is necessarily in-
complete.

BENEFITS OF A LIBRARY STORAGE FACILITY

Increased Seating for Students

Erosion of seating areas due to bookstack encroachment will cease, and some lost seating will be replaced.

Improved Collection Management

Books in the open stacks will be thinned sufficiently to provide ample space for new acquisitions and for efficient reshelving of materials.

Improved Access to Materials

Storing low use materials will make it easier for the user to locate items sought among the remaining volumes. Factors contributing to this increased ease will be fewer shelving errors, increased distance between shelves which will allow the shelving of some folio volumes with the regular collection and the elimination of the fore-edge shelving of books, and better control over the materials on the shelf - all concomitants of having to shelve considerably fewer volumes in a given number of linear feet.

Protection of Materials

It will be possible to move from the open stacks to the security of the storage facility significant numbers of volumes whose value dictates that they should be held in a restricted access area.

CURRENT STATUS OF THE STORAGE FACILITY

The State of Washington has put off making a decision on the University of Washington's request to construct a library storage facility. The Governor, upon receiving the request in late 1974, decided to delete it and substitute a request to the Legislature to fund a study to determine "the feasibility (of) and alternatives to a library materials central storage facility for both public and academic libraries." Three factors contributed to this decision:

1. Two library capital construction projects were submitted to the Governor for approval for the 1975-77 biennium, one by the Washington State Library for a building addition, the other by the University of Washington for a book storage facility.
2. The Governor was aware that the other state-supported university and one of the colleges are considering additions to their main libraries and that the Washington State Advisory Council on Libraries has been looking into the storage needs among all libraries.

3. The State has been actively working toward centralizing functions to improve efficiency and to promote equality of treatment.

The Legislature subsequently approved funding for the study, which is to be coordinated by the Washington State Library and completed in time for consideration during the 1977 legislative session.

Thus the desire of the State to determine the total library storage needs of the state and to meet them in a comprehensive, coordinated way has made the future of the proposed library storage facility at the University of Washington extremely uncertain. It appears that the solution to the library's space problem, already at a crisis level, will not come soon.

DISCUSSION

Question from the floor: I understand that Harvard did a study to determine the percentage of the collection used frequently, that is, used within one year. I was wondering whether anyone was concerned with the relationship between studies like that and the kind of storage configuration.

Walsh: I am personally not familiar with such a study done at Harvard, but that's not to say that that didn't take place. There is the Fussler-Simon study at the University of Chicago which was published in 1969; a statistical sampling of the collection was done there. At Harvard, in several cases where the entire class was seen as little-used, but still worthy of being kept for research value, we decided to move to the Deposit Library entire sections of the classification scheme, such as encyclopedias, directories, juvenile literature. Large numbers of varying editions of titles were also moved. Many decisions were made and continue to be made at the point of selection; so that, when a book selector decides that the item fits within the collection, he attempts to make a decision on its use; and it is automatically classified for the Deposit Library, never going into the Widener stack. Similarly, commitments were made in journal selection so that the volumes, as they continue to accrue, go immediately to the Deposit Library and never enter the main bookstack.

Metcalf: There was a study made of the use of the books that Harvard sent to the Deposit Library some five years after that building was opened, and it was found that the average use of the books in the Deposit Library was 1% as much per book as those that were left in Widener. Now they were very carefully selected, and the use of books in a storage library depends, of course, on the selection. At Harvard the practice, during my time at least, was whenever a serious student objected and said that a book he required shouldn't be in the Deposit Library, we moved it back into Widener. There were only a handful of cases of that kind. The principal difficulty came after the Library of Congress mission from which Harvard received, the year after the war, some forty thousand volumes that it was unable to get because of the Second World War. They were sent more extensively than others. Some of the professors got very much provoked because they had never seen the books on the shelf. When they got the books, they were not interested. I might add that a quarter of the bulk of the books in Widener in 1942 were moved to the Deposit Library. The total use of those books was only a handful a day. They were all in the catalog with the proper classification and could be obtained within twenty-four hours, or you could go over, a fifteen-minute walk, and use the book yourself at the library. But I can assure you that no group of college professors will ever be satisfied with any selection in the Deposit Library.

Walsh: I might just point out, two of the first elements that we used to cut our teeth in data processing are seen as merging, by happy accident, to give us a sense of what really is used and what isn't. The first use of data processing in the college library was a circulation system. We can take this data base at the end of the year and print out titles most used in each classification. Since the Deposit books are preceded by a "K," we can ask the data base to tell us how many K-items went through a transaction over a certain number. This then tells us those items that perhaps ought not to be at the Deposit Library. Reversely, the second element of our use of the computer was to put our shelf list in machine-readable form. We now have about a ten-year data base of circulation statistics. If we were to merge the shelf list, which is 60% complete, and the circulation records, they would tell us where there was not a hit. We would then have by call number those items that did not move at all in the past ten years. When the shelf list is completed, one of our thoughts is to do this. We will then actually know what is moving, what isn't, and what ought to be in Deposit and what, perhaps, ought not to be there.

Tjaden: I see the point of the question that the gentleman asked: if a book were shelved in ordinary call-number order, in stacks that are seven shelves high, what would its circulation be; and if it were shelved by size in a remote area, what would its circulation be; and what is the comparison of those two rates of circulation? To my knowledge, no study of that sort has been done. We know how things are used in storage, but we don't know how they might have been used had they been in regular call-number order in a public-access stack.

Metcalf: Florabelle Ludington, before the Hampshire Inter-Library Center was started, made a study of the use of the books in the Mount Holyoke College Library, which was a good, well-selected college library. She, of course, had no way of knowing what books had been used at the shelves, but they found that one-half of the books in the library had never been used by anybody.

William J. Kirwan (directed to Tjaden): My question concerns the cost figures between standard shelving and compact shelving. Also, did you say that you found a 25% difference, regardless of the arrangement of the books on the shelves?

Tjaden: Assuming the same arrangement on standard shelving as there was on the compact shelving, there was always a 25% differential. Whether books were shelved in regular call-number order, which generates a 20-volume per sq.ft. capacity on standard shelving, or whether they were shelved by size, generating a 64-volume per sq.ft. capacity, the compact shelving still represents a 25% differential. I based the figures on an estimate from one supplier of electrically operated compact shelving, and an estimate of standard shelving costs. However, I should point out that yesterday it may have cost $90 for a double-faced section of standard shelving and tomorrow it might cost $50; that happened to us at the University of Washington last year. We paid $50 for a double-faced section when we bought 240 double-faced sections, so everything is a little squishy. However, it seemed to me that the electrically operated compact shelving was always more expensive.

Kirwan: Did you also include the per-square-foot construction cost of building? You mentioned several factors; what were those factors?

Tjaden: The construction cost and the cost of the shelving - that was all. I used those two, because Lee Ash in his book *Yale's Selective Book Retirement Program* used those two figures.

Question from the floor: (Indiscernible)

Walsh: We're just one of the members or renters of the New England Deposit. That million capacity is not available solely to us. We are the largest renter. We pay $10,000 a year rent which is about half of the total income every year, so we're occupying about half of the space at this moment. The Deposit Library itself is expandable, on a multiple of six; five more stacks the size of the existing one can be built if the members so decide. I doubt if that will happen in the near future. We have expanded into the New England Deposit Library. Several original members have pulled out as they built larger new libraries on their own campuses. Boston University is no longer a member; Simmons College is no longer a member. Harvard, M.I.T., and Boston Public are the three big renters, and they've carved up the space that others have vacated. The complexity here is that the membership is for the Harvard College Library, which is the main library for the Faculty of Arts and Sciences, and the other libraries of the system cannot rent space in the New England Deposit Library without becoming members. There is a lot of legality here, and it has to do with the way the system is organized. For example, the Law School, the Education School, the Divinity School, pretty much have had to go it their own way.

Novak (directed to Tjaden): If the State of Washington decides to consolidate all storage for both public and academic libraries, do you envision that the site that you have chosen for your storage library will be used for this consolidation? Or do you think that the State will pick another site, perhaps a different location, perhaps with large acreage for greater expansion?

Tjaden: I would be very much surprised if it were sited where the University of Washington anticipates siting its storage facility. It would have to be somewhat larger, I would imagine. I guess we're still hopeful that the requirements of the university are so different from the requirements of the public libraries that the legislature will see fit to allow the university to have its own facilities. But, just off the top of my head, I would say no. If it were a central facility for the entire State, it would not be located on the campus of the University of Washington.

Marjorie Rhoades (directed to Walsh): About membership in the Center for Research Libraries, we're beginning to wonder if it makes sense to build regional and state storage facilities. Aren't we really talking about a national center for lending on the order of the National Lending Library in England? They have hardly ever had a conflict with two people wanting the same thing at the same time.

Walsh: I think this is certainly a trend that is developing; it's in this program as a topic later in the session. I know there are proposals, especially in the scientific disciplines, for a national periodical library here in the United States on the order of the Boston Spa. It comes to the theoretical question: if you know where an item is bibliographically, isn't that solving much of the problem, rather than having it right in your own house? It's a poor scholar who can't wait two days for an item.

Rhoades: We can get things from the Center for Research Libraries quicker than we can get them from Boulder, which is only forty miles down the road.

Metcalf: When the New England Deposit Library was started well over thirty years ago, we had ten different libraries. No two of them were similar in character, and Boston had for many years tried to avoid unnecessary duplication between these libraries. We found practically no duplication in the little-used books sent from Harvard, the State Library, which sent a good many, the Boston Public Li-

brary, the Boston University Library, and various other libraries
of different character. A very different situation occurred at
what was the Midwest Library Center and is now the Center for Research Libraries, where the principal members in the original
group of ten or eleven were quite similar state university libraries. They had a tremendous amount of duplication where they were
able to dispose of material to advantage. This is the important
point. If you have libraries of different character, they do not
have less-used books of the same kind; but, if you have similar
libraries, you will get a good deal of duplication.

I want to speak of one other matter, the question of cost of
a storage library and of compact storage. There is no question
in my mind that if you wanted extra space on Wall Street in New
York where space is worth - well, twenty years ago it was worth -
a thousand dollars a square foot, compact storage is worthwhile.
The largest compact storage in the world, until recently, that is,
within ten years, was a Nissen hut in Australia that cost $1.50 a
square foot for that hut, an old army hut. They had bought the
most advanced type of compact storage, automated and electrified,
and were so pleased with saving space that they couldn't get over
telling the whole world about it. When the New York Public Library started its second storage building on West 43rd Street,
they put in a great deal of compact storage, but that was thirty
years ago when space cost a good deal less than it does now.
They decided that their compact storage cost more than the space
that is saved. Now that would not be the case today, because
space in New York City is so much more expensive. The time is
approaching, certainly with the increased cost of building, when
compact storage will be cheaper, unless its cost increases at the
same rate. We need to have another study made on the subject,
such as the one Bob Muller made twenty years ago.

Leo R. Rift: We haven't directed ourselves very much to college libraries,
and I would like to point out that, although one college library
was mentioned where 50% of the books had never been used, that
was very unfortunate. In undergraduate work, the book that is
not seen will not be used. The bibliographic access alone does
not work. Now we, if we are careful, hope to acquire books that
will be used. We are selecting and we are directing the acquisitions and the use by our students. We might say that it is a
kind of positive censorship of selection, but we have to maintain
that. In my particular case, I know that in some areas where our
curriculum was not particularly strong but where the demand for
material appeared on the increase, the curriculum sometimes followed our acquisitions. So use is not always the proper criterion.

Are microforms an answer/ partial answer to library space problems?

INTRODUCTION

In discussing any alternative to running out of space, the alternative has the potential of creating more problems than it solves. Because of the numerous problems already encountered by libraries in the use of microforms, it is necessary to assess the ramifications of a large microform program for library services, for acquisition and equipment budgets, and for the responsiveness of the collection to traditional patron needs. More and more pressure is being exerted on librarians by university administrators and state budget officers to economize on space by turning to microform. Unfortunately, the problem that is raised by this proposed economy was not fully addressed by the speakers. The problem is, essentially, the requirement to acquire duplicate copies of existing holdings in microform. This emerges as a problem for different reasons, depending on whether acquisition of microforms is being considered for retrospective collections or for current acquisitions.

Retrospective Collections

If the library collection is a mature one and the library is out of space, acquiring titles already in the collection on microform to avoid constructing new building space would be a major economic undertaking. A major portion of a retrospective collection would not be available on the commercial microform market. To convert a retrospective collection into microform, therefore, would cost at least $18 per volume. For 20,000 volumes the cost for conversion would be in the neighborhood of $360,000. If one made the decision instead to construct a building, with

21

stack space only, to house these volumes at a liberal cost of $100 per square foot, the total cost of new construction would be $139,200, 61% less than to convert the collection to microform. Add to these comparative costs the fact that few people are willing to invest scarce funds to convert low-use material to microform and the fact that funding for microform is normally part of the library book budget while funding for building construction is usually specially allocated funds separate from the library operating budget, the case for conversion of retrospective collections to microforms is difficult to support. The problem is that too few advocates of microform conversion are aware of these cost implications.

Current Acquisitions

The second problem relates to current collections, limited to serials because, apart from government documents, few new publications are published in microform. As a matter of fact, there are very few serials which are published in microform. For those that are, most publishers require that the paper copy be purchased in addition to the microform edition, the latter at 40% the cost of the former. Serials budgets are already strained to the point that subscriptions are being dropped. How can one justify buying a microform duplicate of a current journal for the purpose of saving that elusive item, space, unless the binding cost savings are equal to or greater than the cost of the microform? The publishers need some prodding to make microforms a more feasible alternative for current acquisition. Perhaps a solution to the copyright issue will help to solve the library's space problems.

Moderator's Introduction

John Vasi, Assistant to the Director for Facilities Planning
State University of New York at Buffalo

My present position at the State University of New York at Buffalo involves the planning of new library facilities. We are, perhaps, the last vestige of the Rockefeller administration commitment to the expansion of higher education facilities in New York State. At SUNY Buffalo we are in the middle of construction of a $650 million campus, approximately five miles from our old campus.

We have encountered many problems common to higher education today, such as our continual extending of the completion date of the new building. The campus was originally to be completed in the early 60's; it now looks like the late 70's is a more reasonable estimate. We have had a projected decline in enrollment since the building master plan was completed, a reduction from 30,000 students to 25,000, requiring a reduction in total building space for the campus. Since some of the buildings have already been built, this creates a number of problems for us in adjusting the existing space for departments planned for relocation but whose build-

ings have been cut from the future plan. The third problem that I'm sure
you've all encountered is the general inflation which has eaten away at
the amount of square footage that we can build with the original allotment
of dollars which has not changed.

I think our greatest problem, however, is that the Bureau of Budget
in Albany has decreed that there will be a two-million volume ceiling on
program capacity for any single university center such as ours at Buffalo.
By the time we fully occupy the new library buildings in 1977, or perhaps
1978, we will have reached a collection size of over 1-3/4 million volumes.

We frequently receive suggestions from university administrators for
our problem of running out of space because of the ever-growing collections
and the obviously finite bookstacks. The first solution that is suggested
is throwing away the old books, something that we obviously don't want to
do on a large scale. The second solution is increased acquisition of microforms, a solution that university administrators seem to hear about constantly.

Robert Asleson, president of Xerox University Microfilms, will discuss microform acquisitions as an alternative to hard-copy purchases. Following Mr. Asleson, Susan Nutter of the Engineering Library at M.I.T. will
discuss M.I.T.'s experience with a large-scale microform program. Susan
Nutter's presentation will be especially interesting to many of us who have
not had experience in user reactions to a large microform operation.

Microforms
as an alternative to building

ROBERT F. ASLESON
University Microfilms

Of increasing urgency for libraries in the
United States, and other countries as well, is a
satisfactory solution for the storage problem.
The number of books, periodicals and newspapers
which must be saved for future use is rapidly ex-
ceeding the physical capacity of the buildings
now available or likely to be constructed.

That seems an appropriate opening statement for a 1975 ALA preconference on the building problems faced by American libraries. You
may also find it more than a little interesting to hear that this o-
pening statement is a quotation from an article written by Eugene
Power, the founder of University Microfilms, which appeared in a 1951
issue of *American Documentation*. The alternative of microfilm as a
substitute for binding journals, and as an alternative to building
additions to libraries, is not a new one. The problem has been with
us for a long time, and the potential of microfilm as a solution to
the problem has been recognized for a long time. This article introduced the equation for determining storage costs of bound journals
and microfilm that is the basis for storage cost studies being made
today.

If microfilm does have economic advantages for storing library
collections, and if the solutions have been with us for so long, why
are we here today discussing it as a potential alternative to building,
and as one of many other alternatives?

It has been 25 years since University Microfilms started its service for providing journals on microfilm. In the 1930s and 1940s microfilm was primarily looked upon as a technique for preserving newspapers which, because of the perishable paper upon which they were
printed, were readily identified and accepted as material suitable for

24

microfilm storage. Microfilm was also primarily thought of as making rare materials from distant libraries, such as early printed books, manuscripts, and so on, accessible to scholars in this country.

During the Second World War, University Microfilms was commissioned to film German technical journals which were of interest to the Allied scientific community. This program provided insight into the ways in which film copies of journals might be used, and led to an awareness of the potential for converting journals to microfilm as a storage medium for libraries.

The original concept was that rarely used journals which were taking up space in library buildings would be the prime candidates for microfilm. University Microfilms was aware of the tremendous costs of storing these rarely used paper copies, and so, in the 1950s, initial attempts were to obtain permission to film rarely used journals. We soon found this was not the right strategy because the journals most in demand were the popular ones. And so, after initially working on obscure journals like the *Australian Sheep and Goat Raiser,* attention turned to the popular journals such as those published by Time, Inc., Newsweek, McGraw-Hill, and others.

The growth of this program was extremely slow, and acceptance of microfilm by major libraries in this country as a substitute for binding was not high.

During the 1960s a number of developments occurred which have had a marked impact on the acceptance of microfilm in more and more academic libraries. Because of the tremendous influx of new college students, the number of new colleges, and thus the number of new libraries, increased substantially. Microfilm was the only viable alternative for many of these new libraries to use in starting their collections. Older established institutions also were faced with the problems of coping with more students and expanded course offerings. These libraries, in many cases, had not subscribed to those journals which were now essential for their academic programs, and so extensive retrospective buying of microfilm was the only option available to them.

At this same time, and for the first time, the federal government launched programs to help build the collections of academic libraries, and many of the materials wanted by these libraries were available only in microfilm. For the most part, these buying decisions by libraries were not really made with any consideration of the economies of storing film as opposed to storing the bound volumes. During the 1960s, academic libraries enjoyed the greatest building boom ever, and very few librarians were bringing to the attention of their funding sources the difference in economics between storage on film and paper.

Today librarians throughout the United States find themselves in a different set of circumstances. Inflation, uncertainty about federal support for collection building, level or falling enrollments have all conspired, resulting in a situation where proposals for additional library construction are being put under very close scrutiny. We are now at a point where libraries of all sizes are looking at microfilm as an alternative to building and are investigating ways in which they can use the economics of microforms as a solution to one of their most pressing problems.

So much for the background - what are the economics of microform for libraries? Any discussion of practical economics means using numbers, and the present case is no exception. Today I must talk in generalities and averages. However, the numbers are meaningless unless their relationship to each other, their source, and the way they are put together are understood. To provide this understanding we have, over the past couple of years, developed a Serials Management program which systematizes a way to look at the economics of serials on microfilm. Our systems analysis takes into account all of the many variables in different libraries and the dynamics of the situation.

Initially I felt pretty good about coming out to Charles Hitch country and talking systems analyses with all the implications of the PPBS, that is, Program Planning and Budgeting System, which Mr. Hitch installed at the Defense Department during Robert McNamara's regime, and which he then brought along when he came out to California to become Chancellor of the University of California. However, I just recently read an article which indicated that the PPBS technique is not really "in" anymore and has gone the way of so many magic formulas for success. Nevertheless, I am sure that the theory behind the program and the good aspects of it have not been lost on administrators and librarians who realize that the operations of a library require a concern for the economics of the system. The microfilm systems studies which we conduct are designed to provide just one tool in evaluating the storage alternatives facing libraries.

A first requirement in any systems study is to determine all the parameters. Another key element in developing systems approaches to a common problem faced by institutions in many different places is to allow maximum flexibility for local variations. The parameter sheets that have been developed for analyzing microfilm as an alternative to binding, and as an alternative to building, list 26 variables which are plugged into a computer program that allows each one of these variables to be changed to allow for local variations. As a result of these computerized systems studies, we can show your library staff the economics of storage costs, replacement costs, acquisition costs, and so on, over a given time period that would result from converting to microforms.

One output of the systems study is a match quotation which compares your holdings file, your wants file, your binding file, or any other file a library contains to the list of materials on microfilm. This quotation enables the program objectives of your library to be studied against a backdrop of the economics of microfilm as an alternative to current storage methods. The systems analysis enables a closer study of the binding and building alternatives.

What are the results of these systems studies, and what do they show us in terms of the economic advantages and space-saving implications of microfilm as an alternative to binding, and the resultant impact on building programs? You can buy a journal on microfilm, with all it takes to read and store it, for

    1. no more than the cost of binding the paper copy, and
    2. less than the cost of building space to house the paper.

You can store a journal on microfilm for less that 4% of the maintenance costs of storing the journal as a bound volume. And you can do this while always having the paper copies in the library during the time of heaviest use.

These are the premises on which the economics of serials on microfilm are based. Here are some practical examples which illustrate the conclusions from these premises:

Example 1

Storage Costs per Volume

The total annual cost for storing a journal volume in conventional shelving is approximately 50¢. This figure includes the cost of space and maintenance costs. This figure is derived by updating the original studies done by Eugene Power, and the later work done by Jeffrey Raffel and Robert Shishko in their *Systematic Analysis of University Libraries* published by the MIT Press in 1968. Literature from vendors indicates that compact storage units require 40% of the space of conventional shelves, so annual storage costs are cut to 20¢ per volume. Since microfilm requires less than 1/25 of the space needed for conventional shelving, annual storage costs per volume are under 2¢. Equipment costs for these alternative storage systems are approximately $1.00 per volume for shelves, $1.50 for compact storage units, and 60¢ for cabinets and readers for microfilm.

Cumulative storage costs per volume for a 10-year period are thus $6.00 for a bound volume on shelves, $3.50 for a bound volume in compact shelving, and 80¢ for a microfilm volume stored in a microfilm cabinet. In addition, of course, would be the installation charges for these three different types of equipment. For shelves and microfilm cabinets this is fairly straightforward, but in some instances can be quite expensive for automated compact shelving units. On a percentage basis costs per volume are reduced 40% by going to compact shelving and 90% by going to microfilm storage.

Example 2

Ten-Year Storage Costs for 2,000 journals

Let's take the per volume costs of Example 1 and determine the 10-year cumulative storage costs for 2,000 journals stored in these alternate ways. Remember, a basic premise of our system is equality between the cost of binding a journal and buying a microfilm copy of that journal.

Adding 2,000 journal volumes per year means that at the end of 10 years storage costs for 110,000 volume years will have been incurred.

Based on the storage costs developed in Example 1, the decision to bind and store 2,000 journals per year on conventional shelves will result in 10-year storage costs of $75,000; a decision to bind and store 2,000 journals per year in compact shelving

will result in 10-year storage costs of $52,000; and a decision
to not bind but buy microfilm will result in 10-year storage costs
of $14,200.

Actually, it is our experience that binding a journal results
in from 1.5 to 2 bound volumes. Using this conversion factor for
our example of 2,000 journals gives even a more favorable economic
result for film. Based on two bound volumes per journal raises
the 10-year costs for conventional storage to $150,000 and the 10-
year costs for compact storage to $104,000.

Example 3

The previous examples show the costs of alternative methods
of storage when the decision is to bind or not to bind journals.
The savings resulted from a tremendous reduction in the size of
the building needed to store the collection.

In Example 3, the savings resulting from converting bound paper volumes to microfilm compared to the cost of building an addition to house the paper will be determined.

One of the basic premises of the serials system analysis is
that you can buy a microfilm volume for the cost of the building
to house the bound paper volume. What do library buildings cost?

In his academic building report which appears in the 1972
Bowker Annual, Jerrold Orne reported that for the five years beginning January 1, 1967, expenditures totalling $984,919,000 had
been made for academic library projects. What did our academic
libraries gain for that expenditure of almost one billion dollars?
According to Dr. Orne's statistics, they gained storage capacity
for 127,377,000 volumes which represents a cost of $7.75 in build-
ing expenditures for the storage capacity for one volume. During
that same period of time, the number of volumes added to the collections of American college and university libraries increased by
100 million volumes, or 80% of the capacity built during this five-
year period was used for additions to the collections made during
that same period. A better analysis for the purposes of our program today is to look at the cost and increased book storage capac-
of library additions. Dr. Orne's report indicates that additions
result in more assignable space and a better return for the dollar
in terms of increased storage capacity than result from new building programs.

During the five-year period 1967-1971, $63,000,000 was spent
for additions, resulting in an increased storage capacity of
11,000,000 volumes, or close to $6 per volume, compared to the
$7.75 per volume derived from looking at total building costs.
The $63,000,000 spent for additions added 2,280,000 sq.ft. of
assignable space, or an average of just under 5 volumes per square
foot.

What has happened since 1971? Mr. Orne's report in the 1975
Bowker Annual indicates that $23,300,000 was spent for additions
in 1974, resulting in 696,000 square feet additional assignable
space, and storage capacity for 2,900,000 books, which converts

to construction costs of $8 per volume, and storage density of
slightly over 4 volumes per square foot.

Based on these statistics, let's assume you have 300,000
bound journal volumes and are evaluating the alternative of building an addition to store them, or converting to a microfilm storage system. Dr. Orne's 1975 report indicated that in 1974 it cost
$8 per volume to build additional storage capacity. This is e-
quivalent to the average price for a journal volume on microfilm,
and so the outlay necessary to convert the 300,000 volumes to microfilm and to build a building to house 300,000 volumes are the
same.

What about the savings in maintenance costs by going to a microfilm system? Although Dr. Orne's figures indicate that additions result in a storage density of about 5 volumes per square
foot which would require a 60,000 sq.ft. addition to house 300,000
volumes, let's assume the square footage required for storage of
the bound volumes will be 30,000 sq.ft. based on the generally
accepted average of 10 journal volumes per square foot. Updating
Raffel and Shishko's 1968 analysis indicates $2 per square foot
for annual maintenance costs. At this rate, annual maintenance
costs for the addition would be $60,000 or $600,000 for a 10-year
period.

For storage of the same information on microfilm using Xerox
Space Saver cabinets which hold 300 volumes per square foot, a total of 1,000 square feet of space would be required, or annual
maintenance costs of $2,000 per year. Thus, the annual savings
realized by converting to microfilm as an alternative to building
an addition would be close to 20¢ per volume per year, or $580,000
over a ten-year period.

These examples have indicated that impressive cost savings can result
from converting to microfilm storage. Let me repeat the source of the parameters which have gone into the determination of these savings. There
are three principal sources:

1. Published studies by authorities such as Keyes Metcalf, Ralph
        Ellsworth, Raffel and Shishko.

2. Academic library building statistics as reported in the *Library
        Journal* and the *Bowker Annual*.

3. Customized systems analyses conducted using a computerized pro-
        gram from figures supplied by hundreds of academic and pub-
        lic libraries.

Each library faces unique conditions when evaluating these alternatives. It is essential that our systems analysis be conducted with due regard for local variations to see where in the spectrum of potential cost
savings your institution falls.

At this point you are probably ready to agree that the storage density
of microfilm is much greater than that of bound journals - even if the
bound journals are stored in compact storage devices. You might even be

willing to concede that building costs for library additions are high, and getting higher, and that the cost per volume stored in new additions is equal to the acquisition cost of a microfilm volume.

Why, then, isn't everyone jumping on the bandwagon instead of just beginning to look at this as an alternative? Why is it that only when under severe financial constraints are libraries giving more attention to the use of microfilm as an alternative? No pun intended, but the major hindrance to wider acceptance of microfilm has been its bad image. The libraries that have been the most successful in utilizing microfilm as a substitute for bound volumes have been those that have treated films just like any other medium.

The Dean of Library Services at Central State University in Edmond, Oklahoma, Gene Hodges, describes their attitude as follows: "Knowledge is knowledge. We don't care if it's bound in cloth or paper or leather or between boards, or if it's put in a box."

The difference between the willing extensive use of microfilm at Central State and the approach found at many other institutions is attitude. The microform reading room at Central State is not a separate room, but is the periodicals room. No distinction is made between the students' use of and access to bound, unbound, or film copies of journals and other serials. A student using bound, unbound, or film copies of the same journal finds them all in the same place, on open shelves, and with reading facilities in close proximity. Central State and other major users of microfilm have exploded the myth that currently available microfilm viewing equipment is unacceptable. They have met the challenge of the need for instructional programs for users and for maintenance programs to make sure that the equipment is always in top-notch order. They have also met head-on the potential negative user reactions that are so often called show-stoppers by some institutions. The attitude of library staff and administrators is the key to the successful installation of a serials management program utilizing microfilm. I would encourage any of you who can to visit Central State University. It epitomizes the potential cost-saving of microfilm, while enhancing the operational effectiveness and attractiveness of the library.

We have all seen the dungeons and attics where microfilm has historically been stored. That approach to microfilm turns off students, faculty, library staff, administrators, and, unfortunately, even your microfilm salesman. As a part of our systems approach to improving the utilization of microfilm, University Microfilms provides design services where we work with you and your staff in helping to design the environment that can replace crowded, cumbersome stacks and prolong the life of your current building. We do this by providing a new library - without a new building.

The current buzzword in library circles seems to be accessibility. Every issue of a library journal has at least one article in which the author is advocating the steps which should be taken to promote accessibility. The microfilm reading rooms were designed so that the film, the reference materials, and the reading stations were in close proximity, easily accessible to patron and staff member. Imagine the effectiveness in operating a circulation and reference service using journals where everything is laid out in such a way that staff members can be simultaneously aware of what is happening at the desk, in the reading spaces, and in the stacks.

Tied to the accessibility question is the problem of mutilation. In some libraries replacement costs for damaged or stolen materials siphon off 5% of the materials acquisition budget. The costs for buying replacement pages or issues, and rebinding them in a bound serial volume (or replacing a missing bound volume with a reprint or photocopy) are very high. Microfilm storage of journal materials minimizes the mutilation and replacement factors, and as a direct consequence improves the accessibility of the material needed by your patrons. True advocates of the PPBS technique mentioned earlier would insist on assigning a lost opportunity cost to measure the effect of every situation where a patron is denied access to desired material because it has been removed from the bound volume. I don't know what value you place on that category of cost, and so I will leave it to you to decide when you are assigning variables to your customized system analysis.

Arnold Toffler has made us all more aware of the inevitability of change and the ever-increasing rate of change. University Microfilms believes that as inevitable as the change from '75 to '76 or from inches to centimeters, is the change from bound volume to microfilm.

User preference studies of microfiche: The M.I.T. Project Intrex and Barker Engineering Library experiences

SUSAN K. NUTTER
Massachusetts Institute of Technology

Microform systems have traditionally served the major purpose of space compaction, and their value as a medium for storage is obvious. However, the success or failure of the utilization of microform systems as a solution to space problems lies in the response of the user. If the use of microforms is limited due to a negative attitude on the part of the user, microforms are not an effective solution for libraries. The possibility that the historically observable preference of library users for text on paper would continue to assert itself after much of the material stored in library collections had been converted to microform[1] led Project Intrex to include user preference studies measuring the acceptability of microfiche among its many experiments.

Project Intrex was a program of experiments intended to provide a foundation for the design of new library systems for universities in the decade of the 1970s. Between 1965 and 1973 this group of faculty, staff, and students at the Massachusetts Institute of Technology "undertook a broad program of experimentation to learn how university libraries might provide better access to recorded technical information."[2] The program focused on the improvement of conventional library procedures through the application of technical advances in data processing, textual storage, and reproduction and the organization of information transfer communities based on time-shared computer systems.[3]

Project Intrex envisioned the future uses of microforms playing an active role in the information transfer process. The microform as a medium for both storage and transfer of information had important implications for library network and resource sharing applications. The traditional role of microforms had reflected an administrative solution to the problems of acquiring and storing specialized materials, which had resulted in a limited number of applications and, therefore, a limited and exceptional use pattern and user group. It was obvious that the user clearly preferred the text in paper form to the text in microform. If

the medium were applied for its own merits, accompanied by serious attention to the needs of the user, the result could be a utilization of microforms that would benefit both the library system and the user. Project Intrex hoped, in its user preference studies, to provide a model
that could demonstrate for research libraries some possible steps to be
taken in the transition from traditional library services to those having
a strong dependence on micromaterials.

Project Intrex had established a "model library" in order to provide
an environment for the performance of its many experiments. MIT's Barker
Engineering Library had been chosen to serve as the model library environment. It operated outside the MIT Libraries as an experimental unit
in which innovative approaches to information transfer were tested.
There, experiments could be tried, competing technologies investigated,
new equipment tested, and methods of service evaluated. The actual library users with their very real information requirements would provide
valuable feedback. For, only by setting up and running a pilot system in
an operational library environment, and thus meeting and coming to grips
with real, everyday problems, would the Project be able to assemble the
experience required to evaluate its experiments.

Microfiche was chosen as the microformat for the user preference
studies. It was a particularly amenable format for the engineering collection of the model library. One characteristic of the microfiche gave
it a significant advantage over the other forms: the one-to-one relationship between a microfiche and a document. Consequently, the storage
and retrieval of any one unit is simple and straightforward. Automatic
selection and retrieval would also be possible with microfiche since
unitization is the key to the successful application of a microform information retrieval system. The publishing industry had also recognized
the advantages of microfiche and seemed to be leaning toward the use of
microfiche as a dissemination medium for a considerable portion of its
future output. Furthermore, the System Development Corporation had recently completed a study for the National Advisory Commission on Libraries to evaluate and determine the trends in microform, the probable usage of microforms as a storage medium over the next 20 years, and the
most promising and dominant microformat for libraries.[4] The results of
this study led the Commission to predict that the dominant microform for
library applications would be the microfiche sheet.[5]

The choice of microfiche allowed for experimentation with the "duplicating library" concept. (The duplicating library concept is limited
to microfiche, because only fiche-to-fiche cuplication is economically
feasible for microform consumers.) Because microfiche is a low-capacity
microform, it is the most appropriate dissemination medium (except for
aperture cards) for supplying "on demand" copies of single units of information to meet specific user requests. In the duplicating library the
microfiche is never circulated. Instead, it is duplicated on demand
through diazo or vesicular fiche-to-fiche copies, and the user receives
his own non-returnable copy of the material. The library copy of the microfiche never leaves the file, and it is, therefore, readily available
for the next request.[6] It is more economical for the library to meet
multi-user demands for the same item by making and distributing cuplicate
microfiche. It is actually less expensive to give away a microfiche copy

than it is to circulate a book because the costly labor expenses are reduced.[7] The library may or may not charge the user for his copy. The
copy can be given to the user as an overhead item instead, for charging
the individual can involve costly bookkeeping.

The availability of circulating microfiche readers in conjunction
with the "duplicating library" concept is to the user's advantage as
well as the library's. The user has the freedom to use the microfiche
wherever he chooses, rather than be limited to the confines and time constraints of the library. The library can reduce the number of expensive
stationary readers and space-consuming reading areas required.

Another, very important variable of the "duplicating library" concept is that of guaranteed access. Guaranteed access had not yet been
carefully evaluated and measured as a factor that could have tremendous
impact on user acceptance of microforms. If the user experiences a low
retrieval rate when using a library, his trust in and support of the library drops. The library could rebuild the user's confidence and support
if it could guarantee immediate access to documents in the collection.
Guaranteed access can be provided efficiently and economically through
the use of microform copies, while it is impractical, expensive, and
probably ineffective, to provide file integrity by purchasing an additional hard copy of every book in the collection.

The planning for the design of a microform environment for the serv-
icing and storing of the microform collection in the model library coin-
cided fortuitously with the major renovation of the Barker Engineering
Library. This afforded Project Intrex the opportunity to design the area
to meet its specifications and needs rather than be forced to create a
microform area through makeshift adaptation of some expendable, although
perhaps totally unsatisfactory, space. The Project Intrex staff worked
closely with the architectural firm of Skidmore, Owings, and Merrill in
the planning for the physical rehabilitation of the circular Barker
Engineering Library, so that the design would permit the integrated performance of two functions: conventional library service and experimentation with new forms of information transfer. It is pertinent to note
here that the library occupies 35,000 sq.ft. on five floors, accommodates
250 users and 75,000 volumes, and is staffed during a ninety-two-hour week
by seven professional librarians and twenty-four support staff. As well,
the library has an off-campus storage facility for older and less-
frequently used materials. The library's collection supports the research
and teaching activities of the 2,300 students and faculty in the School of
Engineering.

The Microform Service Area was planned so that in design and operation it would provide an optimum physical and psychological environment
for the utilization of the collection. The design followed a systems approach that had as its central focus the needs of the user. The importance of the principle of systems design in microform planning cannot be
emphasized strongly enough. Most microform applications in libraries have
failed to grow due to a lack of systems design, and the loose application
of systems components in libraries has frequently resulted in prejudice
against the entire concept.[8] It is also important to note here that the
initial development and application of user-oriented systems require financial resources that are outside the realm of the annual library budget, particularly since few libraries have adequate research and develop-

ment funds. Therefore, unless there is an initial outlay of financial resources to provide for a systems approach, a library runs a high risk of a negative user reaction.

The Microform Service Area was located centrally to allow the user easy access. It was given priority space on the main floor of the library adjacent to the central reading room and therefore escaped the all-too-frequent relegation of microform areas to the remote and dreary basements of libraries where the users are forced to work in semi-darkness and isolation.

The environmental conditions of the Area are the same, except for lighting, as are found in any well-designed library area. The facilities were designed for the comfort and the service of the user and the protection of the microforms. The lighting in the Area is fully adjustable, and the acoustical requirements for reduced noise levels were met, as were those requirements for temperature, humidity, and air flow for "intermediate" or "sub-master" copies.

The Microform Service Area occupies approximately 1,000 sq.ft. The duplicating library concept eliminated the need for a significant amount of space devoted to reading equipment and their respective study carrels, since portable fiche readers were made available for loan.

In March of 1970 the Barker Engineering Library opened its Microform Service Area, and the Model Library Project embarked on the user preference studies that continued through June of 1972.[9] On opening day the collection consisted of only a few hundred titles on microfiche: the documents comprising the Intrex data base, selected technical report literature, some MIT School of Engineering theses, the *Thomas Micro-Catalogs*, and a few selected current journal titles. At the end of fiscal year 1970/71 the collection had grown dramatically by 10,000 titles and 35,000 sheets and was expected to continue that rate of growth in succeeding years.

A substantial effort was constantly directed toward a publicity program of displays, demonstrations, mailings, etc., calling attention to the advantages of microfiche. Bibliographic access identical to that for documents in hard copy was provided by cataloging all microfiche with the same rules as their hard-copy counterparts.

The Area was staffed during every hour that it was open by a person from the library's support staff. The person selected for staffing the Area was one who had a positive attitude toward microforms, based on experience with the medium. It was suspected that acceptance of microforms by the user might be partially dependent upon the attitude of the staff toward the medium, and that a negative attitude would be easily communicated to the user. The staff person retrieved the microfiche and copied it for the user and was available for assistance in using the variety of reading equipment. In addition, careful maintenance of the equipment and the proper storage and handling of the microforms were important responsibilities of this staff member.

Service to readers was provided through the use of the following commercially supplied equipment:

1. A microprinter capable of producing hard copy from negative microfiche.

2. A microfiche printer and a microfiche processor which in combination provide on-demand fiche-to-fiche copy service in approximately 30 seconds.
3. Five stationary microfiche readers.
4. A carousel filing system, a power-driven rotary microfiche file with capacity for 50,000 titles.

The stationary readers had specially designed carrels to accommodate them and to provide for both left-handed and right-handed note-taking. Each member of the staff involved in the processing of microfiche had his own reader.

The general objectives of the user preference study were to provide access through microfiche to the text of documents held by the model library; to provide access to the text of documents in either microfiche or hard copy, with the user making the choice of form, under suitable restraints or controls; and to provide a closely observable environment in which the user's preference and other relevant reactions could be observed and recorded. Differential fees were used as variables to test the strength of user preferences. From the experiments it was hoped to derive conclusions on microfiche acceptance that are valid, at least, for the students, faculty, and research staff that use a technical research library.

From the outset, guaranteed access was stressed. Each user received a duplicate microfiche copy of the item requested. The library's fiche was then returned to the file, ready for the next request. The user was given the option of retaining the fiche copy at no charge or having hard copy produced at charges varying from $.10 per page to free. It was this choice that the Model Library staff studied in order to determine user preference between microfiche and hard copy at varying costs as well as which variables affect that preference.

In the first calendar year of operation, 1970, the use of the Microform Service Area was low, and the sample of users was too small to indicate significant trends. There was no evidence to change the widely held view that the majority of library users have a strong preference for hard copy over microform copy when both are equally available. The users cited as their primary reason for preferring hard copy the lack of microfiche reading equipment outside the library. In order to obtain the level of usage commensurate with the costs of operation and the needs of the study, the Model Library staff believed that the collection would have to be developed and expanded in both size and comprehension, and that extensive advertising of the availability of the microfiche would be necessary. At this time an 8-pound portable microfiche reader, developed under the sponsorship of the Office of Education, became available in quantity to the Model Library Project. The experiments in loaning these readers would give the opportunity to test the view that the use of microfiche will increase in proportion to the ease of availability of portable readers.

The next six months (1/71 - 6/71) saw a substantial increase in the use of the Microform Service Area. The increase appeared to have resulted from three factors:

1. Growth of the microfiche collection.

2. Substantial publicity efforts.
3. Acquisition of portable microfiche readers for loan.

It is significant that the breaking point signalling the increase in use came immediately after the portable fiche readers were first made available for one-week loan. The percentage of users choosing microfiche was 91% while 9% paid $.10 a page for their hard copy. The reasons given for the preference for fiche included the convenience in size and storage, immediate access, the higher cost of hard copy, and the availability of portable readers. Those users preferring hard copy indicated they did so primarily because they lacked reading equipment outside the library, because they needed to make frequent referrals to their documents, and because they disliked fiche.

The next six months (7/71 - 1/72) saw a continuation of the trend of continually increasing usage of the Microform Service Area. This period showed that the preference for microfiche over hard copy had risen to 95%. The comments elicited from users showed this increase to be the result of two factors:

1. The users were more aware of microfiche's convenient size and
       advantage in storing.
2. The users were more comfortable in the use of microfiche.

The lower cost of the microfiche was no longer cited as a significant factor; instead, it was important to the user that microfiche is compact and that access is immediate and guaranteed. The small number of users who continued to prefer hard copy still cited the same reasons, but there was a large drop in the number who cited the lack of available reading equipment outside the library. By this time, a number of users and a number of MIT Laboratories had purchased their own microfiche readers. Another interesting piece of data gleaned from the user study was that the percentage of users choosing the hard copy at $.10 per page remained constant until the document length reached 100 pages; after that point all requests were for fiche.

At the end of this reporting period, the use of the Microform Service Area had reached a level where it was possible to shift microfiche and hard copy costs in order to test user preference at various cost levels. On December 6, 1971, the cost of hard copy was reduced to $.05 per page. This price remained in effect for an experimental period, after which the hard copy was made available at no cost so that the absolute preference between microfiche and hard copy could be determined. An artificial time lag was introduced for the availability of microfiche copies so as to equal the time period that existed for the availability of hard copy, so that the experiments would not be weighted in favor of the microfiche.

The next six months (1/72 - 6/72) marked the end of the user preference study. During this time the use of microfiche increased substantially. It is important to note here that the microfiche collection had also increased substantially during the study, and that by the end of June 1972 it had grown from a collection of several hundred titles to a collection of approximately 22,000 titles representing almost 60,000 sheets of microfiche. The two cost ratios were studied. When microfiche was offered at

no charge and hard copy at $.05 per page, 93% of the users still pre-
ferred microfiche. This represented only a 2% decrease from the last
period when hard copy was $.10 per page. There was a more significant
decrease when microfiche and hard copy were both offered at no charge.
However, 80% still preferred microfiche, while 20% preferred hard copy.
Of those 80% who selected microfiche, 84% said they did so because of
the convenience. There is another very striking statistic to be examined here. When analyzing the data for the period when both microfiche
and hard copy were free, the preferences of the previous users of microfiche were isolated from those who had never before used microfiche.
The results were surprising and exciting: of the previous microfiche
users, well over 90% continued to prefer microfiche to hard copy even
when hard copy was available free of charge.

It is appropriate here to look at the cumulative statistics for the
use of microfiche during the entire Model Library study - from the opening of the Microform Service Area in March 1970 to the completion of the
user preference studies in June of 1972. During that period a total of
2,086 user requests were filled. Of those, 1,888 or approximately 91%
were for microfiche, and 198 or approximately 9% were for hard copy. The
statistics on why users selected microfiche indicate that the convenient
size of the microfiche played the largest role in that selection:

> 45% cited the convenience of microfiche
> 30% cited the lower cost of microfiche
> 10% cited a curiosity about microfiche
> 8% cited the immediate availability of microfiche
> 7% cited miscellaneous reasons

The 9% preferring hard copy gave as their reasons the following:

> 50% cited the lack of microfiche reading equipment outside the
>   library
> 20% cited the need to frequently refer to their documents
> 11% cited a dislike for fiche
> 19% cited miscellaneous reasons

Throughout the study the users reported their reactions to the reading equipment for microfiche, and their overall response was reassuring.
87% were satisfied with the equipment, and only 13% had complaints.[10]
That was three years ago. What has happened since then? The Microform Service Area was an experiment that was so successful in a real environment that it could not be terminated. The users had become so accustomed to the service that it was essential to them that it remain available after the experimental project had accomplished its purpose. The Microform Service Area became an integral part of the Barker Engineering
Library's operation.
The Library has continued to keep statistics on the use of the Area,
in order to insure that the user's needs continue to be the focus of the
operation. While the user preference statistics have been discontinued,
others have been added in order to determine, in addition to level of use,
to what extent the different types of material in the collection are used,

who the users are, how much it costs to provide duplicate microfiche copies, how users find out about the availability of a microfiche copy, etc. Because there are time constraints, and because many of these findings are limited in relevance to engineering collections, only a general and brief overview of current microfiche use will be presented here.

The statistics indicate that the Microform Service Area is a very successful user service. Since the last year of the Project Intrex experiments, the number of user requests has grown a dramatic 600%. Approximately 9,000 documents in microform are requested annually, and approximately 20,000 sheets of microfiche are duplicated. Furthermore, the use of the microfiche collection, relative to its size, is almost identical to the use of the hard-copy collection, relative to its size. This significant increase in use has been brought about primarily through collection development efforts and publicity programs.

The microfiche collection has grown just over 200% since June 1972 to a collection of approximately 47,000 items, representing about 100,000 sheets of microfiche. It is now one-fourth the size of the hard-copy collection and is composed of all of the types of material contained in the hard-copy collection.

The development of the collection has been aggressive, following the same policies established for the hard-copy collection. It has focused on recently published, high-use material. In general, the Library has avoided large-scale acquisition of retrospective material and overnight conversion of segments of the collection. The day-to-day experience with users in the Microform Service Area has dashed any expectations of altering user behavior patterns in a direction or at a rate that the user will not accept. The Library, however, did do some large scale, in-house microfiching, at the beginning of the Intrex experiments, of some unique materials in the collection, whose availability in hard copy was somewhat limited to the users. The trend toward simultaneous publication in microfiche and hard copy has expanded the opportunities for collection development and has brought about many of the changes in use pattern. It is apparent that when the materials in microform are generally consistent with limited usage - o.p. material, storage, archives, preservation - the use of them is exceptional; while when the materials in microform are of a current and relevant nature, the use of them is broad and routine. Therefore, the aim of the Library's microfiche collection development is no different from that of its overall collection development - to provide a current research collection of continually changing content that is constantly reviewed and weeded, so that it always reflects the current research and teaching activities of MIT's School of Engineering.

The cost of giving microfiche copies to the user, at no charge, has averaged approximately $1,400.00 per year or approximately $.075 per microfiche sheet.[11] In relation to the Library's total budget, this figure is not significant. The Intrex studies suggested that if a library charged the user for fiche copies, the charge should approximate the actual cost to the library of providing that service. The studies indicated that this charge would fall somewhere between 10¢ - 25¢ per microfiche sheet, depending largely on demand. On April 1 of this year, the Administration of the MIT Libraries effected a change in the Barker Engineering Library's policy of giving microfiche copies to the user at no charge.

The user is now required to pay 10¢ per microfiche sheet. The effect of this policy on demand is being carefully monitored.

Staffing the Area has not required the addition of any personnel. Total user service time averages between two and three house per day. This time is divided between two members of the support staff whose regular job responsibilities can be easily carried out in the Area. Careful evaluation and reallocation of work responsibilities as well as optimization of work procedures have allowed the absorption of this time by the staff. Since the microform collection is integrated bibliographically with the hard-copy collection, there has been no increase necessary in reference services to the user.

The user preference studies and the subsequent Microform Service Area experiments clearly indicate that microfiche is an acceptable information format for engineering library users when certain conditions are fulfilled and that, when given the proper environment, this acceptance can develop to such a point that microfiche is actually preferred over hard copy by a majority of users even when the document is offered simultaneously in both forms at no cost. User acceptance will enable libraries to take advantage of the space savings of micropublications, thus increasing the storage capacity of present library buildings and postponing the construction of additional storage space.[12] The essential elements which make this enthusiastic acceptance of microfiche possible are a microform environment that is as comfortable as conventional library areas; a current, relevant collection of material accessed through the card catalog; close attention to the quality of the microfiche in the collection; modern high-quality readers and reader-printers in sufficient numbers; portable microfiche readers for loan; and an aggressive publicity program.

REFERENCES

1. Carl F. J. Overhage, "Introduction," Massachusetts Institute of Technology. Project Intrex, *Project Intrex*. *Semiannual Activity Report*, PR-7 (Cambridge: Massachusetts Institute of Technology, 15 March 1969), p.1.

2. Carl E. J. Overhage and J. Francis Reintjes, "Project Intrex: A General Review," *Information Storage and Retrieval* 10 (May/June 1974), p. 157.

3. Full documentation of all of the Project Intrex experiments is contained in Massachusetts Institute of Technology. Project Intrex, *Project Intrex*. *Semiannual Activity Report*, PR-1 through PR-14 (Cambridge: Massachusetts Institute of Technology, 15 March 1966 - 15 September 1972).

4. Arthur A. Teplitz, *Library Fiche: An Introduction and Explanation* (Santa Monica, California: System Development Corporation, 1967).

5. Douglas M. Knight and E. Shepley Nourse, eds., *Libraries at Large* (New York: R. R. Bowker Company, 1969), p.623.

6. Lawrence B. Heilprin, "The Economics of 'On Demand' Library Copying," *National Microfilm Association Proceedings* XI, 1962, pp.311-339.

7. Teplitz, *Library Fiche,* p.4.

8. Peter R. Scott, "Appendix K. Project Intrex and Microphotography," in *INTREX, Report of a Planning Conference on Information Transfer Experiments,* ed. Carl F. J. Overhage and R. Joyce Harman (Cambridge: M.I.T. Press, 1965), pp.203-214.

9. The funding for the Model Library Project was met by a grant from the Council on Library Resources.

10. More complete and detailed statistics of the user preference studies are contained in Massachusetts Institute of Technology. Project Intrex, *Project Intrex. Semiannual Activity Report,* PR-10 through PR-14 (Cambridge: Massachusetts Institute of Technology, 15 September 1970 - 15 September 1972).

11. This figure includes only the costs of replaceable materials.

12. General estimates of space savings of microform over hard copy range from 94 per cent to 98 per cent for microfiche and from 85 per cent to 98 per cent for microfilm.

DISCUSSION

Tjaden (directed to Asleson): In view of the report to the National Advisory Commission on Libraries, to which Susan Nutter referred, noting the ascendency of microfiche, and in view of the University of Washington's preference for microfiche over microfilm, even for periodicals, what is the attitude of University Microfilms toward producing microfiche?

Asleson: Well, notwithstanding what you might be reading in the press, we are moving toward microfiche; we have been producing microfiche for many, many years. We will move forward in microfiche production just as fast as we can develop the technology that's required; that's really what it boils down to. There are still some technology problems that we have in the production situation. I am speaking now of the need at the current time to film things twice in order to be able to provide it in both formats. Our attitude and the attitude that we have expressed in our catalog for the last several years has been that we are committed to getting ourselves in a position where you will make the choice. You will decide whether you want roll film or microfiche. There are advantages to both. Nutter's program will not work in an open stack situation. The example I use is a 300,000-volume collection of journals. If that were converted to microfiche, with possibly five to six fiche per volume, you would have millions of cards requiring the type of system that Project Intrex has, which is a closed system, and which works very well in that type of environment. It would not work well, I feel, in open stacks. In your card file, you have a little rod that goes right through the bottom of all the catalog cards, because you have found that you cannot have your catalog card file in a situation where the users have the ability to pull the cards out. We do now provide this format and will be providing more and more material in both formats. It is our objective to reach the position where you make the choice, where you decide what format you want, as I have said before.

Question from the floor (directed to Asleson): I was wondering, in helping librarians design microform reading rooms, if Xerox has developed any sort of formula or rule of thumb for deciding the number of microform readers required either per user or per volume or in some combination.

Asleson: Yes, we have. I think it's one reader for every 500 students - that has been what we have used in some of our analyses. We also have some other systems that we've worked out for people with use of one reader per 2,000 volumes on film as a rule of thumb. But here again, I must stress the fact that the decision must be made locally. We have variables we can crank in; we have experience factors we can talk about. The best one, of course, is Central State, which has made a total commitment to microforms. Whenever it is possible to buy something in microform, they do it. And their user experience has been our primary resource.

Question from the floor: I wondered if you were monitoring any of the results besides Central State.

Asleson: I can't say that we have any studies going that would satisfy the rules and regulations of a scientific experiment, but we certainly have close touch with the major users. As more and more libraries now convert and become major utilizers of microforms, we talk to them and watch them very closely because we need the feedback.

Vasi (to Nutter): I think you were telling me about a ratio of readers to microfiche readers which circulate.

Nutter: Right; of the portable readers, we have one for every 250 students, but that's not enough. We have reserves on the readers. We're having some problems with support from our present administration for more readers. They have a somewhat different attitude toward microforms than our particular library has, but they haven't had the same professional experience with microfiche for a variety of reasons. One for every 250 is not enough. I'm not sure of the number, but a very large number, I might even say 500 of our students and laboratories and faculty, have purchased their own microfiche readers and constantly come to us for consultation about which reader to buy and where they can get it. Basically, what they want is the cheapest and for their own use are willing to take a reader that does not necessarily have the best optics but is cheap.

Steve Schneid (directed to Asleson): You indicated 6,000 sq.ft. of floor
          space providing for 62,000-volume capacity. Maybe I wasn't
          listening carefully, but was that to indicate that that area has
          6,000 sq.ft. and that area could house 62,000 volumes?

Asleson: Yes.

Schneid: This is conventional shelving. In laying out conventional shel-
          ving in a 6,000 sq.ft. area, I can provide a working capacity of
          96,000 volumes and an overall capacity of probably 150,000 in the
          same area.

Asleson: This is what I mentioned very briefly. I realize that this be-
          comes more controversial with individual librarians and with in-
          dividual situations. I think that in this situation we find the
          greatest range of what is actually happening in library facili-
          ties today; what is the actual capacity to be gained per volume
          per square foot? You must remember that I am talking journal
          volumes; I don't know if the numbers that you just quoted are
          journal volumes, monographs, or all materials.

Schneid: Conventional book volumes, overall.

Asleson: With journal volumes, of course, you get a lower capacity per
          square foot than you would with monographs, government documents,
          and that type of thing. This has been one of the things that
          we've had the greatest trouble with in trying to work out our
          system. I was very encouraged to hear Ms. Tjaden talk about the
          wide range of shelving prices that they had received. That's
          been the one thing that, every time we get new information, just
          seems to throw our previous studies out. I can see now that
          there is a tremendous variation from quotation to quotation, even
          from the same vendors, for things like shelving. There is no
          hard-and-fast rule; there's no ironclad number of parameters you
          can plug into our equation. It does require sitting down with
          each of you, finding out your experiences, finding out what your
          own situations are, and determining what the potential savings
          might be for you.

Rift (directed to Nutter): Your project's a very successful one, but it
          has one limitation. What have you been doing about the copy-
          right? Now when you duplicate microfiche and when you sell that
          microfiche, even non-profit, then you're really on thin ice.

Nutter: I agree with you. We are opposed to charging for microfiche.
          The M.I.T. administration decided to charge, and they said they
          would assume full responsibility, so we had no other choice.
          One of the advantages of an engineering collection is that a
          great deal of the materials are not copyrighted. When we copy a
          journal, we try to limit it to the article. We have the student
          write down exactly which pages. The students sign for everything

they take. They write down exactly which pages they want; and they can't have a whole issue of a journal even if they want it, unless they are willing to state that they really want to use every single article in the journal. We try to protect ourselves that way. This is how we keep our statistics; in the same way they sign out for a book, they sign out for the material. There has been nobody really trying to collect whole runs of journals. A lot of the other material we have is out of print, and the copyright has expired.

Rift: The student can keep that duplicate or does it have to be returned?

Nutter: He keeps it.

Rift: He keeps it. Well, that's like taking away the book.

Nutter: He has the option of using it in the area at no charge and also returning it. One of the advantages, of course, of microfiche is that a student can build a compact file of references in his subject area that he can easily carry with him. It's a lot cheaper than circulating a book, that's for sure.

Valerie Rohrbaugh: I understand that it can cost from $4.50 to $5.00 to convert a document to microfiche originally if you have to do it yourself. I wonder if you'd comment on how much of your material was available from publishers on microfiche and how much you had to do yourself and how you obtained the funding to do it yourself.

Nutter: First of all, Project Intrex Model library experiments were funded by a grant from the Council on Library Resources. They provided us with funds to do some in-house, large-scale microfiching. We chose to make microfiche copies of every M.I.T. School of Engineering thesis from 1945 to 1971. We also have a storage facility where all of our journals and serials previous to 1950 are stored. The high-use materials there are also microfiched. Most of the other material we have been able to buy from publishers. Of course, we get a lot of technical report material. We find now a lot of university presses are offering microfiche editions; a lot of the regular publishing companies are offering microfiche editions. An interesting thing occurred with the theses. When 1971 arrived and we didn't have any more money to do the fiching, the students decided that they wanted all the M.I.T. libraries to have theses on fiche. They decided that they would pay for it themselves. They have to turn in, when they turn in their dissertations for B.A., M.A., and Ph.D., the original copy plus a duplicate copy which they pay for. They decided to turn in a regular copy and a microfiche copy, so that the students are now paying for the microfiche copies.

Nutter (in response to a question on equipment): There is one thing that we found which we didn't expect to find. We did some studies to try to find the universal reader. We found that every single reader had a user who liked it so that we have a wide range of readers; we don't stick to one type.

Metcalf: I'm very enthusiastic about the use of microfilm. I don't want to talk about myself, but I was fortunate enough to be in charge of the first use of microfilm in a library in the United States, just as I was in charge of the first photostat machine in the United States. However, there are two or three things that we need to keep in mind about it. Even Harvard with its nearly 10,000,000 books uses more space for readers and service for readers and non-assignable space than it does for books. We're not saving as much as would be indicated in space. Second, the readers themselves who use the microfilm or microfiche take more space than others. They require more service if you have closed access material, and it has to be passed out. If it is open access, it is much more in danger, particularly with the portable readers available, of loss than books are. Finally, the percentage of material in the large university library that is available in micro-reproductions of any kind is comparatively small. Microfilm, microfiche, microprint are available only as additional material, on a small scale, of course, not as large as for books. I suppose Harvard has at least three million, and probably five million books, that will never be put on microfiche or microfilm; and space will have to continue to be available for them.

In an undergraduate library where the material would all be available or could be made available on micro-reproduction, I think that the undergraduate students would probably do better using the hard-paper copy that is purchased, rather than to provide reading machines for each of the thousands of seats. I don't want to discourage anything that's been said today, but it will not completely solve our problems.

Julian Michel (directed to Nutter): You've indicated that there are two options, one for microforming and another one for conventional storage. Is any policy developing locally about the relationship between the use of those two options?

Nutter: I'm not sure I understand what you mean exactly by "a policy."

Michel: Theoretically, if microforms are becoming acceptable to the user, it ought to be possible to plan for a situation in which you will not need conventional storage for hard copy. So, that leads me to wonder whether you are looking forward to the possibility of getting rid of your conventional storage, and my practical reason for asking the question is that I have been dealing with conventional storage for about ten years.

Nutter: We've considered this, and the M.I.T. Library administration has not been willing to make a policy to allow anything to be discarded in hard copy. We have a new director coming in September, so we're expecting many changes. We really feel that we want both; that microform alone is not an alternative, that there are certain journals which have to be retained in hard copy and certain books that have to be retained in hard copy. There are certain kinds of materials that are amenable to the microformat. We also combine this with a very aggressive weeding program, so that we try to reach a balance. I don't think microform is the only answer.

Michel: Have there been any situations in which you have been able to take something, a specific title from the storage library, convert it to microform satisfactorily, and then eliminate the hard copy?

Nutter: Yes, we decided to do that with about ten titles, but then we were not allowed to withdraw them.

Equipment affecting space utilization

INTRODUCTION

New equipment may help librarians to utilize existing space more efficiently, but it may also require new building space with new spatial configurations to house it and new types of mechanical-electrical systems to operate and maintain it. With such stringent requirements as the 300 pounds per square foot floor-load capacity needed for compact shelving, for example, the new equipment and technology will increase the difficulty in continuing to utilize many existing library buildings.

As Frazer Poole has noted, compact shelving is not new, but new technology has been applied to an old concept, and there are now several shelving systems available on the commercial market. However, the need for this benefit must be substantial to justify the increased economic investment and the decreased access to the material stored on these shelves.

What Harold Roth has called "automatic compact storage" provides even greater efficiency in utilization of book storage space. It has, however, two major drawbacks:

1. It requires a building space, approximately 41' 4" high by 73' 4" long with each module width of 9' 11 1/8", dimensions not readily accommodated in existing buildings; and it requires a floor-load capacity of approximately 200 pounds per square foot.
2. The technology for the automated retrieval system as specified for Nassau County is not yet operational anywhere.

Librarians look forward to the future installation of such a system at Nassau County Research Library, so that they will understand the operational and housing problems associated with it.

The new CISTI library building in Canada utilizes a variety of new technologies to resolve numerous library problems. The building has been planned for no expansion, but that is dependent on future warehouse storage. Perhaps warehousing will not be necessary if microforms and magnetic tapes can come to the rescue in the next 15 to 20 years.

Compact shelving

FRAZER G. POOLE
Assistant Director for Preservation

The problem with talking about compact stacks in any detail is that it takes a great deal more than our allotted twenty minutes. Thus all I can do this morning is to talk in general terms and provide some details about the proposed Library of Congress installation.

During this conference, which has been titled "Running Out of Space - What Are the Alternatives?" we have heard about one alternative - the possible use of microforms in certain circumstances. Now we turn to a different alternative. Certainly in an era in which librarians have seen building costs rise from $15 to $20 a square foot to $40 and $50 and more, it is logical to study the possibility of increasing book storage capacity by the use of more efficient shelving. It is, of course, well known that shelving arrangements traditionally used in libraries are wasteful of floor space and generally inefficient for the storage of books. The usual system of fixed stacks and aisles by means of which books are accessed utilizes only 30% to 35% of available book storage space in our libraries. Compact bookstack designs on the other hand, in contrast to the traditional system of fixed stacks and aisles, make it possible to achieve a utilization of floor space which may range from 50% to 75% or more. Expressed in another way, it is possible to obtain an actual increase in shelving capacity ranging from 75% to 100% by the use of compact bookstacks instead of standard bookstacks. In the new James Madison Memorial Building of the Library of Congress, for example, the use of compact bookstacks will make possible a 90% increase in the book storage capacity of the Law Library collection area.

Now this preamble is not to suggest that in any way compact bookstacks are the answer to every library storage problem. Such is not the case, and this paper will try to review both the advantages and disadvantages of compact bookstacks, as well as the special circumstances in which they may offer a viable solution to certain storage problems. At this point let me say that the figures given above for the more efficient utilization of floor space or greater book capacity will vary with each situation, depending upon the design of the compact bookstack selected, the building module, the size of the columns, the type of material stored, and other factors. One can make some generalizations as to cost, efficiency, and capacity, but every storage problem must be analyzed in terms of the specifics of a given situation to obtain the actual results.

Compact bookstacks, in one form or another, are not new. Librarians have been seeking more efficient ways of shelving their collections for at least a century. One of the earliest solutions to the problem of more efficient book storage was that of Charles Virgo, an English librarian, who in 1878 developed a compact storage shelving design used in the Bradford Free Library. Virgo's device consisted of a movable bookcase hinged to a stationary bookcase. Books in the inner case were accessible only by swinging open the outer case in a movement very much like opening a door. Virgo's cases were used in Bradford until 1903. However, there seem to be no reports of this design being used elsewhere in England, and it appears that the installation was something less than a total success. The original cases, however, were fabricated out of wood; and it may have been the wood which caused the problem rather than the design itself. In fact, the same design, with bookcases fabricated in steel rather than wood, was used in several libraries, both in the United States and abroad, over a period of the next fifty to seventy-five years.

This design, in which one or more movable cases are hinged to a fixed or stationary range, is usually referred to as a revolving compact shelving design. Units may be double-layered or triple-layered, depending on whether the movable unit is single-faced or double-faced. In this design, a wide variety of combinations and arrangements is possible. It is interesting to note that for some seventy years most revolving bookstack installations were made in the United States. By 1958, however, the revolving design had gone back to Europe, had been introduced into France, then was used in other countries. In the United States, the most notable example of revolving or hinged compact shelving was the installation produced by Sneed and Company for the Midwest Inter-Library Center; now known as the Center for Research Libraries. This installation, made in 1951, is still in existence, and appears to have worked well. I understand, however, that in the expansion of the Center for Research Libraries new designs are being investigated as a possible substitute for the old Sneed revolving shelf design.

Although the exact date is uncertain (at least I have been unable to find it), the sliding-drawer design for compact storage appears to have been developed considerably later than the revolving or hinged case design. This design bears little resemblance to standard book shelving since it utilizes different principles. Basically, the sliding drawer design uses a complex and costly stationary steel frame into which the book storage units, which are little more than open drawers, are inserted. Usually each drawer contains two rows of books back to back. Other configurations have been used, although as far as can be determined there is very little difference in the efficiency of the two systems. Best known in the U. S., sliding drawer shelving has also been used in Russia and in some other Eastern European countries. Apparently it never caught on in western Europe. This shelving as far as is known is no longer made in the United

States. The best-known manufacturers of sliding drawer compact shelving were the W. R. Ames Company, which produced the "Stor-Mor" design, and the Hamilton Manufacturing Company, which produced "Compo-Stacks." Both firms have now gone out of business, Hamilton having gone out of the book-stack business, although it still manufactures other steel equipment. Some other manufacturers in the United States, Shelco was one, have pro- duced similar units. Sliding drawer designs have a number of disadvan- tages including lack of direct access. Although used to some extent, this design never achieved any widespread acceptance.

A variant design, once made in the United States, was called "Conserv- a-File." In this scheme movable shelves were hung on tracks in front of fixed regular shelving. The outer row of shelves contained one less shelf than there were sections in the range. By moving the front shelves to the left or to the right as needed, the books on the inside shelves were ex- posed and accessible.

Sliding or rolling compact shelving in one form or another is almost as old as the revolving or hinged case type, dating to before World War I. Three basic designs have been used. So far as can be determined, however, only two of these are manufactured today. These designs can be described as parallel sliding or as perpendicular sliding, depending upon whether the movement of the cases is parallel or at right angles to the longitudi- nal direction of the ranges. The first sliding compact shelving of which there is record was installed in the Bodleian Library at Oxford. Later, similar shelving was installed in the Cambridge University Library. Both installations were products of the British manufacturers W. Lucy and Com- pany. In the Bodleian Library design the cases were of the parallel slid- ing type, although there seems to be no published description of the exact design. When the Bodleian Library was expanded in 1946, this pre-World War I installation was dismantled. The Bodleian cases moved on the floor. However, in one of the storage cases in the "Iron Library" of the British Museum, so called because the stacks were all made of cast-iron, a sliding shelf design was installed in which the sections moved on overhead rails in a direction parallel to the long axis of the ranges. The movable cases were placed on only one side of the original stationary ranges leaving al- ternate sections readily available. This installation lasted until 1920, when the weight of the hanging cases resulted in the failure of the sup- port system. Here we have one of the problems in the use of the compact shelving. The load requirements on the structure are significant and must be taken into account.

A third type of parallel sliding shelving, developed in 1930 by Sneed and Company for the Toronto Public Library, consisted of double-faced sec- tions moving on casters. No tracks were involved. These units were sim- ply parked with the ends against one wall and pulled out into the main aisle when access to the stored materials was desired. These were simply oversized book trucks stored close together.

Of the parallel sliding shelving designs, only those in which single- faced sections move parallel to a fixed range appear to be used today. In the U. S., one manufacturer of this kind of shelving is still in production.

The earliest known use of perpendicular sliding shelving was in the British Museum. This installation was made in 1890 and preceded the par- allel sliding units installed in the Iron Library. Without dwelling fur-

ther on the evolutionary development of such designs, however, let us
take a look at currently available compact bookstacks.

With the exception previously noted, all present-day compact bookstacks utilize the perpendicular sliding case design in which the ranges
move on tracks in a direction at right angles to the ranges. Such stacks
can be manually operated or motor-driven. Variations on this basic design are manufactured and sold in Asia, Europe, and the United States.
Outside the United States, the best-known names are "Elecompack," made in
Japan and sold in this country by the Remington-Rand division of Sperry
Rand, and the Ingold-Compactus, made originally in Switzerland but now
produced in England, France, Austria, and in two or three other countries.
As far as known, Ingold-Compactus has no installations in the United
States.

American manufacturers of compact bookstacks include the Stor-Trac
Division of Product Innovations, Inc.; H. P. H. Industries, Calif., which
markets its design under the trade name of "Magic Aisle;" the Space Saver
Corporation of Fort Atkinson, Wis., which markets its bookstacks as Space
Saver Mobile Storage Systems; the Estey Corporation of Redbank, N. J.,
which markets Estey Compact Mobile Storage Shelving; and Dexion Incorporated, which markets a system known as "Live Aisle" Mobile Storage System.
Lundia, Myers Industries, Inc., markets a system called Fullspace. The
units in this system are built of wood, not steel. In addition to the a-
bove, there are a few manufacturers of similar equipment used for parts
storage in industry. The design of these products is not suitable for
books, however.

Each of the manufacturers of compact shelving for books uses the same
basic design in which a superstructure of shelving unit rests on a carriage supported on wheels which run on a track system attached to or embedded in the floor. The carriage unit may be a motorized unit, or the
whole unit may simply be moved manually. There may be end-panels and a
canopy top. In this design the practical length of the ranges is determined by the size of the motor, the size of the module, and the size of
the area in which they are to be installed. Ranges stand side by side on
a track system and may be moved by a motor or by hand. Such a block of
compact stacks has a fixed range at each end of the block and a single
floating aisle which changes position as the stack block is opened to the
point at which access is desired.

Track systems for this type of compact bookstack vary from the high
profile design of Space-Saver, which looks like a miniature railroad track
and is 2½ inches high, to the medium profile system of Stor-Trac System,
which uses a 3/4-inch round rod for a track, to the low-profile systems
of "Elecompack," "Magic-Aisle," and Estey, all of which have heights of ½
inch or less. In those systems having individually motorized ranges, power is usually transmitted from the motor shaft to the drive shaft and the
wheels by a chain. One design is direct drive.

Space-Saver uses side-guiding wheels to keep moving units in alignment and has a patent on that design. "Elecompack," "Magic Aisle," and
others use flanged wheels for alignment.

The safety features incorporated in the various designs constitute
one of the most important aspects of motorized compact storage systems.
These features should be examined carefully by a prospective buyer. At

one time some instances were reported in Europe, in which people had been seriously injured, or in one case had been killed by the lack of adequate safety devices on compact stacks. These accidents happened more than twenty years ago. Today, safety devices are nearly foolproof in every system.

In the Space-Saver system, the flooring acts as a passive safety device; it disconnects all circuitry when an aisle is in use. This system is considered foolproof, but is somewhat more expensive than other types of safety features, and results in a floor higher than those systems which use low-profile tracks. The "Elecompack" and Estey designs provide full-length safety bars at floor and waist levels. These bars are much like the rubber safety edges on elevator doors and use the same basic principles. This design has an advantage in that the floor-level safety bar can be activated by a book or other object on the floor, thus preventing injury to the object.

The speed at which motorized unit ranges move varies slightly with each manufacturer. The fastest units require about ten seconds to open a three-foot aisle; the slowest require as much as nineteen or twenty seconds. Many designers believe that the optimum time required to open a three-foot aisle should vary from fifteen to eighteen seconds. Movement which is too fast may cause books or other material to slide off the shelves. A speed slower than that required to open a three-foot aisle in twenty seconds may be too slow to permit convenient access to the collections. Control systems range from those which are completely solid-state to those using both solid-state components and mechanized relays or some other combination of electronic and mechanical controls.

The lighting of compact stack units varies from designs in which the lighting is an integral part of the installation to those in which the regular building lighting is used. Most manufacturers, however, offer both systems at the purchaser's option. Both types of lighting systems have their advantages and disadvantages. In a time of energy shortage and high lighting costs, systems which incorporate the lighting in the stack design so that the lights are on only when an aisle is open and in use, obviously offer significant savings in lighting costs. If normal lighting is not incorporated in the building design, and this assumes a new building, the use of the compact stack area for other purposes will be made more expensive by reason of the added costs of installing lights at a future date. On the other hand, it is probably unlikely that a storage area containing a very expensive compact bookstack installation would need to be converted to some other use. If the lighting is part of the stack installation, there is bound to be some loss of flexibility. It is up to the librarian to determine whether this loss of flexibility might be serious at some future time.

Mobile bookstacks impose greater than ordinary stresses on the stack components, thus lateral motion or rocking must be held to a minimum. As a result, some compact bookstack designs embody additional reinforcing units at the outer face of the stack sections. Others use end-panels on each section with reinforcing members on the front edges of the panel.

Floor load requirements must take into account the weight of the bookstack installation plus the weight of the stored material. It has been generally accepted in practice that a floor-loading factor of 250 pounds per square foot is adequate. For some materials, such as phonograph records, however, this is not strong enough and the floor-loading factor may need to be increased to 300 pounds per square foot, sometimes more. Such materials as manuscripts closely packed or materials in which the predominant form is coated stock paper (which weighs twice as much as ordinary book paper) require stronger floors. The final determination of whether a floor in an existing building will be strong enough for a compact bookstack installation can only be made by a competent engineer working with the librarian and the bookstack manufacturer. In many cases the bookstack manufacturer has his own engineer. However, it is important to obtain an unbiased engineering opinion with respect to this problem.

Unlike the situation in conventional bookstacks, where there are few if any patents, several manufacturers do hold patents on one or more features of their compact bookstacks. It is interesting to note that there are several suits now filed or about to be filed in connection with various compact bookstack designs.

Although the subject of this talk was to be compact shelving, not compact storage, it should be noted that a few librarians have tried to solve their storage problems by the use of very narrow aisles, rather than by the use of compact bookstacking systems. The Yale University Library adopted a 22-inch aisle in its storage libraries instead of the normally used 36-inch aisle. In using this system, Yale elected to shelve books on their fore-edge on a pre-sized, fixed location basis. Princeton has used the same method. Whether this would be acceptable in many cases is something that only the librarian could determine, but it should be studied very carefully. As a librarian with a strong interest in the preservation of library collections, I find this practice of storing books on their fore-edges most objectionable, since nothing is guaranteed to damage book bindings quicker than to shelve volumes in this way.

Up to this point the present paper has reviewed various types of compact storage systems and outlined their more important characteristics. Let us now examine some of the basic aspects of compact library storage. Let me say at the beginning that these problems are too complex to be discussed in any comprehensive way in a brief period of time. Librarians who need to understand the problem in its many ramifications should consult the extensive literature on the subject. Fremont Rider, Gawrecki, Ellsworth, Shishko, Muller, and Fussler and Simon should be studied in depth for a full understanding of the various alternatives and the costs and efficiency of compact shelving. It does seem safe to say that no librarian should consider any compact storage system until it is clear that the library is running out of space and until he is willing to give serious consideration to the removal of the least used materials to remote storage. Thus compact storage facilities may well be justified in cases where it is essential to keep reasonably inactive, closed-access collections in a main library building where normal storage space is wholly inadequate.

The Library of Congress elected to provide compact storage facilities for its Law Library collection in the new James Madison Memorial Building only because there was no other way to keep this collection on Capitol Hill, and it was generally agreed that the collection must be readily accessible to users.

The use of compact storage facilities at some location remote from the main library poses still a different problem. No matter what type of storage facilities is used, there will be some degree of inconvenience to the reader. On a university campus such inconvenience is certain to lead to strong objections by the faculty and perhaps by the students. No librarian can make plans for remote storage without the support of his faculty, and this may be difficult to obtain, or it may not, depending upon circumstances. Obviously, however, one factor which will influence faculty in their approval or disapproval of the remote storage facility is retrieval time. A system in which a book can be brought from remote storage to the main library or to the reader in less than one hour will undoubtedly generate more faculty support than the location in which half a day or more may be required to serve the library's users. Faculty members and graduate students generally ask for the books they need. Undergraduates may or may not do so but, generally speaking, tend not to ask for things they can't find. Thus one of the intangible factors in remote book storage is inconvenience to the user about which the librarian may not be well informed.

Much of the inconvenience caused by the use of compact storage derives from the extended retrieval times. A related factor is the question of direct access. If the librarian wishes to provide direct access to the collections for his staff or, on occasion, to the faculty and other special users, he must choose one of the compact bookstack systems described above. Not all systems in which books are shelved by size on their fore-edges in a fixed location permit direct access, nor do such mechanical systems as "Randtriever."

Since the question of direct access may be an important one in faculty acceptance, the librarian should give it very careful consideration. Again, it should be remembered that shelving books on their fore-edges may save space but is extremely damaging to the volumes. Ultimately such damage must be repaired by expensive rebinding. I still remember my utter astonishment when I learned that Fremont Rider not only shelved his books on their fore-edges but actually trimmed them to fit his shelves. It's a little like the fairy tale of the giant and his bed. If his guests were too short, he stretched them; if they were too long, he chopped off their legs. It may have given him a perfect fit, but it was hard on visitors.

Any compact storage system requires that lesser used materials be selected and removed from the general collection and reshelved in the new facilities, whether these be in the main library or at some remote location. As a result, the librarian is faced with a whole series of problems and decisions including: 1) how books to be stored in the compact system are selected, 2) who is going to do it, 3) how much staff time will actually be required, and 4) what the cost will be to change the library records to show the new location, etc. There are many, many problems to be considered before compact storage systems can actually be used. If storage is at some remote location, then retrieval and maintenance costs must be computed and added to other costs. The question of cost has no easy answers.

Most of those who have studied the problem in some depth seem to have concluded that in most cases, when all costs are taken into account, the actual savings are either nonexistent or are so slight as to be relatively insignificant. As a general rule, the higher the cost of the building, the greater the savings. Writing in 1954, Muller concluded that compact book-stacks offered no savings at all until the building costs exceeded $30 per square foot. Today that figure is undoubtedly closer to $60 per square foot. It cannot be emphasized too strongly that the costs and any possible savings can only be determined after the most thorough study. Although such cost comparisons are meaningless unless determined for a particular situation, two sets of figures which have recently come to my attention may be of interest. Case A is that of a university library which required storage for 630,000 volumes. The space required was calculated as 15,000 sq.ft. at a cost of $1,550,000 in compact stacks or a cost of $2.50 a volume in compact stacks and 36,000 sq.ft. at a cost of $1,990,000 or $3.16 a volume in conventional stacks. In this case then there was a decided cost advantage through the use of compact stacks. I have not checked these figures and I do not know the basis on which they were derived.

Case B is a university library which required storage for inactive collections. The cost was calculated as follows: 81¢ a volume in multi-tier stacks, 88¢ a volume in free-standing stacks, and $1.46 a volume in compact stacks. In Case A the cost advantage was clearly in favor of the compact stacks. In the latter case, Case B, the price advantage was greater in the case of conventional stacks or multi-tier stacks. If these two instances show anything, it is simply that individual situations vary so much that no cost generalizations can be safely made.

The foregoing discussion has suggested that compact storage systems should be used only for relatively inactive, closed-access collections. However, some few librarians, both public and academic, have used compact bookstacks for active, open-access collections. No information appears to be available on how such installations have been accepted by users, but most librarians, and certainly I am among them, would argue against such a use of compact storage because of the inconvenience to users.

I have been asked to comment on the proposed compact storage system for the Library of Congress for which we are now in the process of accepting bids. Let me say that we decided to keep two collections (law and part of the music collection) on Capitol Hill. Large though it is, there was inadequate space in the building for these collections without the use of compact stacks. We looked at all the designs available on the market, saw many features we liked, some features we didn't like, and decided that we would design our own. Because the amount budgeted for this installation was large we believed we could get regular manufacturers to fabricate these compact bookstacks to our own design. The design we now have, or rather the design for which we are now evaluating bids, has some advantages over those designs presently on the market.

In the Law Library collection, we will use stack units eight shelves high with shelves twelve inches deep. In the music collection area, the units will be ninety inches high (plus the carriage height) with shelves sixteen inches deep. The latter depth is necessary because we will be shelving manuscripts in fifteen-inch-deep, flat storage manuscript boxes. The Library of Congress design is generally similar to "Elecompack" or to the Estey design but has some special features including louvered end-panels and canopy tops to promote air circulation. It uses three-phase 208-volt motors for greater reliability, full solid-state controls, dual reset buttons, a special safety feature which utilizes solenoid activated brakes on the motor shaft which must be released before the stacks can be set in motion, and low-profile tracks which will be the same height as the finished floor.

In conclusion, I can suggest only this word of caution: compact book-stacks may well provide the best means of solving difficult and otherwise unsolvable space problems. However, librarians should not expect any significant savings in cost; indeed, there may be no savings at all. Only a thorough study of all the factors involved can result in such determinations. Under many circumstances user acceptance may be limited, and the cautious librarian will make certain that he has the backing of his administration and his possible users before he makes the final decision.

A truly automated retrieval system or compact storage a la carte

HAROLD L. ROTH

Director, Research Library County of Nassau, New York

Lee Ash considers himself the greatest solution to the need for compact storage. He also considers himself the world's greatest weeder of collections. In a sense he is correct. The best solution to costly exponential collection growth is a well-designed though drastic program of weeding. Not all libraries are of the same mind, and some libraries, the Nassau County Research Library, for instance, designed to be a backup research facility with a responsibility for current and retrospective collection development, encourages collection weeding for others by growing itself.

This library in its program planning predicted a one-million volume stack collection in its original programming seven years ago with a standard stack construction in mind. The total structure proved to be too expensive for the County to support. At this point another approach was called for to halve the size of the structure. It was felt that the collection size was correct, but the method of housing it might be changed with the advancing state of the art. Culling the literature we found that a truly automatic compact storage unit which might meet the need had been developed by Supreme Equipment and was marketed as Randtriever by Remington Rand. Question of its capacity to house more than 250,000 volumes had been raised. However, it was felt that research requirements called for a management control stack situation which updated the control feature the New York Public Library uses to control its stacks, offered the opportunities for guaranteed location control, accommodated the latest equipment for maintaining use statistics, accepted a mini-computer and circulation equipment, provided a reasonable throughput and a minimum of downtime, offered accessibility from several levels, and provided flexibility as well as delivery to the delivery clerk and automatic return to a returnable location.

A building consultant, familiar with approaches to compace storage, Ralph Ellsworth, was employed to assist in the initial planning and to de-

velop the program. He set up the first meetings with the Library Bureau
people marketing Randtriever and arranged for visits to all of the active
installations in the United States. (There are four at the present time,
two in public libraries in Indiana, one in a community college in Iowa,
and the fourth in the Medical Library at Ohio State University.) All
proved to have fixed location devices with storage boxes of the same size.
The systems essentially provided a stacker assembly delivery process, but
made it necessary to return boxes before calling for a new one. The item
to be returned to the stack required one to call up the box in which it
was originally housed, thus reducing the throughput by half.

Dissatisfaction with the deadheading type of procedure led to a
Trustee's suggestion that the Library try for random storage and access.
Throughput was proposed based on averaging the use of research collections
which maintain statistics. 2,000 uses a day was considered a fair average
of use as was a 10-hour day. NCRL proposed an anticipated doubling the
number of uses and came up with a growth figure requiring a system that
had the capacity to deliver 360 items per hour.

Further study showed that there had been a variety of maxi-load systems (loads over 500 pounds per container used in storage warehouses) and
some mini-load systems (under 500 pounds loading per box for handling
spare parts). However, most of the systems were one-way and were rear-
end loaders, e.g.,

> Philip Morris has a system in Virginia which loads a
> hogshead of tobacco in the back and produces cartons of
> cigarettes in the front. When the hogshead is empty
> they have to replace it with a new hogshead.

None provided for the return or fully automated system we were seeking.
Few producers were interested in designing a system specifically for the
library use envisioned. Once the uniqueness aspect had been overcome,
county engineers did some evaluation and concurred in the necessity in
checking on all possible solutions to the problem and seeing that other
producers of mini-load systems could bid on the proposed specifications.

In conjunction with the architects at O'Brien and Justin and with a
consultant on Automated Retrieval Systems, James Donnellan of East Corporation, a new approach was adopted. The major thrust of the approach was
that the library develop a set of specifications in which suppliers and
producers could bid competitively with a guarantee that the library would
get what it wanted and needed rather than accommodating itself to buying
a system that could essentially be called an off-the-rack purchase.

From that time forward the library talked of this new system as its
ARS, and the staff and all involved became expert on possibilities.

1. It is not unusual to be able to add a computer front end to what
    is essentially a mechanical system, making a storage system
    a management control device.
2. The hardware in which the books are stacked is essentially an
    erector set which houses materials wherever they are put.
3. The computer makes it possible to operate a random access and
    return as well as fixed return.

    4.   Random access will double the throughput of the equipment.
    5.   A 15" bin is not a must. A 36" bin is a possibility.
    6.   Two sizes of bins could be used in the same system.
    7.   A true automated retrieval system where the book comes to you is possible as opposed to a semi-automatic compact storage system where you go to the book.

Additional considerations were those of saving money, saving space and saving on ultimate staff costs and maintenance costs.

The system designed operates as follows:

All the essential actions pertaining to the relationship between storage, retrieval, delivery of books, maintenance of records, and verification of system operation are controlled by a computer.

The computer system enhances the basic library retrieval system by providing: as requested -

> Efficient random storage of volumes
> Circulation and property control features
> Statistical usage data
> Requestor notification/order routing
> Request batching capability
> Monitoring for fault detection

Random Storage

In a random storage system, no fixed storage location is assigned for a given volume. Instead, the volume to be stored is placed in any convenient bin, with the computer memory keeping track of the bin location for each book call number. When the book is called for, the computer looks up the call number to find the bin location where the book is stored, and activates the stacker to retrieve that bin. This random location storage approach greatly increases operating efficiency by virtually eliminating reshelving as a separate task. "Loss" of books due to misfiling is also essentially eliminated.

All book location data are maintained by the computer in a fully secure mass memory, which contains all active call numbers and bin locations, along with other data. (Memory sizes are available covering installations to several million volumes.)

The mass memory locator also provides the capability of indicating to a requestor if the requested book is in use, out for repair, etc.

To facilitate returning books to the stacks (at closing time, for example) and for the storage of newly acquired material, the computer can be instructed to call out a series of empty or partially empty bins from the stacks. The new or returning books are then stacked into the bins, their call numbers read, and the bin returned to the stacks.

Circulation and Property Control

The computer-equipped retrieval system, although not primarily a security system, aids in the security function by providing timely notification of loss of property. This is done by requesting from the computer a list of all volumes which have been removed from the stacks prior to a certain time (or date) and not subsequently returned.

Statistical Usage Data

Two types of usage data are collected by the computerized system. One type is related to usage of the books and the other to the usage of the library.

To monitor and report book usage, the system keeps track of the total number of times that each volume has been referred to, and the last referral date. These data may be periodically written onto tape or disk for processing by another computer, or reports may be generated or inquiries made by the system computer itself. These data will aid library personnel in selection of acquisitions, replacements, and removal of volumes from the stacks.

To monitor the usage of the library, the computer logs and records the total activity level experienced, and the hourly, daily, and weekly variations. Summary reports of this data will aid library management in staffing and schedule decisions, as well as medium- and long-range facilities planning.

Requestor Notification/Order Routing

The computer-controlled stacker system implements the feature by which a customer requesting material is informed when the material has arrived at the pickup station. Typically, the computer would assign a number to the user's "order," and the user would be given this number (say 2 or 3 digits). When the complete order (one or more books) has arrived at the pickup station, the computer indicates this by a numeric display or silent annunciator light display in the customer waiting area.

Request Batching

The system has the optional capability of treating a number of requests together, as a single "order." This is indicated to the system when the "order" is entered.

This means that all items requested are routed to the same picking station, and the picking operator told whether the book taken is the beginning of a new order, an intermediate item, or the last item. Only when the order is complete will the system signal the customer.

Monitoring for Fault Detection

The computer system provides continuous monitoring of the operation and integrity of all components of the total system, including itself. Any erroneous operation detected in the stackers, conveyors, or stations is flagged or alarmed by the computer for corrective action.

Design

The computer system itself consists of an integrated package of mini-computers, CPU, mass memory (disks), and tape or disk backup to the master memory. This provides fully secure non-volatile storage for master files, along with a method for transfer of data from the system to a remote computer. The computer system is compact, reliable, and requires no operator, no special power or air-conditioning, and no attention in operation.

PROPOSED EQUIPMENT

1. 6 aisles 40 tiers high face-to-face columns with capability of delivering at two levels.
2. Bins total 42,000
3. Bin size - 36" x 8" x 10"
4. Bin capacity approximately 24 books
5. Aisle capacity approximately 167,000 books
6. Total capacity approximately 1,000,000 books
7. Approximate module size:
    a. Height - 41'4"
    b. Width - 9'11 1/8"
    c. Length - 73'4"
8. Motor driven belt conveyors equipped with read heads and automatic lateral "push off" capability, to carry the book storage bins from the front of aisle to the librarian control stations.
9. 5 Librarian control stations (2 per level), 1 in basement equipped with input keyboard, read heads, display screens, and buffering area for book storage bins.
10. Patron waiting area equipped with electronic display board.
11. Instruction signs prominently posted so that patron will be able to initiate procedure for obtaining desired book(s)
12. Computer System consisting of mini-computer, CPU, disks, and tape or disk backup to master memory.

Operation of the system provides for

1. Single-book request
2. Multiple-book request
3. Restoring book to system
4. Supervisors' station to control action at each console.

GENERAL

The librarian control stations and the book return station appear on two public levels. One entry station is on the lower level. Each station is completely equipped with all the controls necessary to perform any or all functions. The book return station is equipped with a key which will lock out the "request imput" function during peak periods and may be used solely for returning books and updating the computer. The controls at each station are equipped with "on-off" keys for each function.

During non-peak periods, individual stations may be removed from the circuit by turning the key off. This makes it possible to operate the system with the number of staff dictated by the work load, from the "open" stations. Thus it is possible to have the stations manned with each operator performing independently.

The configuration of the conveyors is such that each returning bin must pass the book Return Station. Because of the ability to refile the books on a random basis, it is possible for the operator to fill all the empty spaces with books being returned before calling for additional bins for storage.

ACTIVITY

In actual operation, the supervisor will have the opportunity to determine how many operators are required at various times of the day and can make adjustments in personnel and operations performed as the work load varies. This flexibility assures a full crew during peak hours and a minimum effective crew during non-peak hours.

SUMMARY

This system is ready to go to bed but has not been tested in this mode yet. Viewing of systems in operation for other purposes shows that this is a feasible method of operation. Systems of this nature, computer operated, are in use in Switzerland, England, and Japan. Most are record systems, but all work effectively and well.

The state of the art keeps developing; and, where reader heads were once used, light pens both fixed and hand-held may be applied. Identifiers which can be read through the cover of a book so that the system may update the location of the volume when returned to the system are also available. Inventory maintenance is almost an on-going process.

The most intriguing aspect of the system is that it is a new form of performing an old job and is the product of the marriage of a hardware erector set and a mini-computer front end which can be cabled to a main frame in and out of house and can adapt to a point where catalog files in data banks can be accessed via CRT's and items ordered for delivery from the system on any level.

CONCLUSION

Decisions to handle or to develop a mini-load system in libraries should be based on need and use as well as on novelty. The economics of the system in question to house and handle 1,000,000 volumes is interesting.

STANDARD		COMPACT		ARS	
100,000 sq.ft. @ $60.00	$6,000,000	50,000 sq.ft. @ $60.00	$3,000,000	6,000 sq.ft. @ $60.00	$360,000
Shelving 30¢-40¢ a book	300,000 to 400,000	*Shelving* $1.30 a book	1,300,000	Cost of system including computer and stacks + or -	2,000,000
Operating		*Operating*		*Operating*	
Maintenance @ $1.50 sq.ft.	150,000	Maintenance @ $1.50 sq.ft.	75,000	Maintenance 1500 sq.ft. and front end Maintenance Man & Parts	10,000 30,000
Staff 45 @ $6,000	270,000			*Staff* 12 @ $6,000	72,000

The cost of electricity and air conditioning are thrown in as having to be considered in either case remembering that the cost to air condition, heat, and light the space for standard and compact shelving would more than balance the cost of operating the automated retrieval system.

While this paper discusses the concept in general of the Nassau County Research Library specifically, the system can be developed after the fact in libraries, as has been the case in Rotterdam, where it is in a lower level area, or in Logansport, Indiana, where a space cube was attached to an existing building. It is a type of system that is flexible and undoubtedly of use in some areas but not in others. A full analysis of the problem is required before a decision is made. This presentation is designed to show and discuss a new alternative to the compact storage problem which has remarkable flexibility and can modernize an arrival procedure to the level of an effective management control device.

There is also more than one practitioner of the art of mini-load systems development, but some are more flexible than others. Supreme Equipment & Systems Corporation has the longest experience in the library and records management field. Rohr Industries, Inc., Kenway, Inc., and Page Airways, Inc., are other companies interested in the field.

The new technology and the design of library buildings

JACK E. BROWN

Director, Canada Institute for Scientific and Technical
Information

Eight years ago, in 1967, the Educational Facilities Laboratories of New York sponsored a symposium in which a group of experts were invited to consider the implications of new technology on the design and planning of library buildings. These experts were asked to consider whether the advances in computer, microform, and communications technology and other related advances called for drastic departure from the traditional lines of library building, planning, and construction. The findings and recommendations of this group were published in a little pamphlet entitled "The Impact of Technology on the Library Building."

During the span of eight years, an era of fast-moving changes, it would seem logical to expect that many technological innovations would have occurred which were unknown in 1967. However, on rereading the pamphlet, I found to my surprise and chagrin that nothing of a really earth-shaking nature had occurred which would nullify or make obsolete the major conclusions and recommendations contained in this report. What has happened, of course, is that the new techniques foreseen or in existence in 1967 have been refined in the intervening years and are now being incorporated into new buildings. Thus, if I had any intention of attempting to bring this report up to date, that idea was quickly dispelled, and I shall limit myself to describing the impact which the new technology has had on a building which was designed to house an organization serving as the focal point of Canada's national network for scientific and technical information services.

Before getting down to brass tacks, or perhaps more appropriately, coaxial cables, and to place my remarks in proper perspective, I would like to say a few words about the Institute to which I have just referred. Such an introduction is particularly in order because of our recent change of name.

The Canada Institute for Scientific and Technical Information (CISTI), a division of the National Research Council of Canada, was established on October 16, 1974, coincident with the official opening of our new building. The Institute, which was created to emphasize the NRC's responsibility for developing a national network of scientific and technical information services, brings together the NRC's two major information disseminating services - namely, the National Science Library and the Technical Information Service, both of which date back to the early 1950s.

Although the name National Science Library has disappeared, the services provided by this organization are being continued and strengthened, with increasing emphasis being placed on the development of new techniques to expedite the transfer or dissemination of scientific and technical information in Canada. For example, national services such as CAN/SDI (Canadian Selective Dissemination of Information) and CAN/OLE (Canadian On-Line Enquiry), both of which are operated on a centralized basis because of cost effectiveness, are being expanded. Equally, since the network is a decentralized one, a special effort is being made to link and utilize for the national benefit, subject expertise and information resources located in all parts of the country.

The other major ingredient of CISTI, namely, the Technical Information Service (TIS), is designed to assist small and medium-sized industry to keep abreast of new developments in technology and research. The bulk of the work is carried out by industrial engineers located in each province who systematically visit industrial firms to identify and assist in the elimination of problems relating to product development and efficient manufacturing processes.

In short, CISTI serves as the major node of focal point in the evolving Canadian network of scientific and technical information services. Its basic aim is to take whatever steps are necessary and possible to ensure that scientists, engineers, technologists, research workers, and managers have ready access to scientific and technical publications and information needed in their day-to-day work - that is, to channel the right information to the right person at the right time.

The initial planning of the building, which now houses the activities and services I have just mentioned, began some thirteen years ago, in 1962. At that time, architects were hired; Dr. Keyes Metcalf was invited to serve as planning consultant; and a group from Ottawa took a trip through the United States to visit large libraries which had been recently completed, or which were still in the early planning stages. Our main purpose was to see how the new techniques for storing and processing information were affecting the planning and design of these buildings. Construction was begun in August 1971, and the building was fully occupied in February 1974.

In designing the building, we tried to meet the following basic requirements:

1. to create a truly functional building
2. provide for maximum flexibility
3. permit the utilization of the latest techniques to facilitate the
        the storage, retrieval, and dissemination of information
4. provide for the logical flow of material and traffic throughout
        the building

5. provide for a growth factor of from 15-20 years
6. provide for the accessing of information by remote means

Again, before getting into technical details, here are a few facts and figures about the building:

the structure consists of a base of three floors in the shape of diagonally adjoining squares surmounted by a square central tower of six floors

the dimensions - 450 feet from opposing corners, 200 feet through the core, and an overall height of 150 feet

built of reinforced concrete, the building is fireproof and is the first structure in Canada to conform to the new earthquake specifications of Canada's National Building Code

the use of light wells and horizontal and sloping skylights over the main public areas provides an overall atmosphere of openness and spaciousness

modules are 27 feet on centres

The gross floor area is 360,000 sq.ft., constructed at a cost of $35 per square foot, including elevators, conveyor system, and shelving, but excluding furniture and art work. The main vertical air ducts which normally form a part of the interior floor space are placed outside the structure, thus giving a much higher percentage of usable interior space.

Now let us consider how some technological advances have been incorporated into this building.

User and Staff Accommodation

For the comfort of users and staff, and to aid in the preservation of books, the building is air conditioned throughout, and designed for a relative humidity of 50%. In order to maintain this high level of humidity without long-term damage to the structure, a construction technique developed by the NRC was employed. This technique, called Rainscreen Design, places a plastic skin over the outside of the reinforced concrete structure, with an air space between the skin and the concrete. This air space is constantly vented and drained so that condensation does not accumulate.

The design of window areas presents many problems - provision must be made for screening direct sunlight and for providing insulation between the work area and the outside environment. The latter is not easy to achieve in the Ottawa area, where temperature differences can be greater than 100°F. These problems were solved by the use of window units with the trade name "Polar Pane." The units consist of two sheets of tempered plate glass separated by a 2-inch air space, with a venetian blind hermetically sealed within the unit. The blinds are suspended on fine stainless steel cables and to maintain the hermetic seal and protect the blinds from both damage and dirt, are operated by a magnetic controller.

The office landscaping or open office concept is utilized wherever possible. In such an environment, a high level of sound absorption is essential. A furniture system was selected in which acoustic panels form an integral part of the desk and related pieces. This arrangement has definite advantages: not only does it eliminate the use of free-standing screens which serve little functional use, but which may cause both lighting and maintenance problems, but it also brings the absorbent surface as close as possible to the noise-generating source. This furniture, being constructed of 122 separate but compatible components, has a further advantage in that it makes the changing or relocation of work stations a relatively simple matter.

While on the subject of sound reduction, I should mention that the ceiling above all of the landscaped areas is of a special design which will reflect and absorb sound within bays and prevent its transmission to adjacent areas. Further sound reduction has been achieved by the use of carpeting on all floor areas in the working environment.

In addition to extremes of temperature, the Ottawa climate presents other difficulties in operating a building having heavy traffic. Snow, which may reach 180 inches per year, with associated sand and salt, is carried into the building. To reduce the maintenance problem to a minimum, large grids with heated sub-surface drains have been installed in the area between the double entry doors, so the slush will be carried away as it melts.

While hardly a technological development, it should be noted that to assist visitors and users, extensive use has been made of supergraphics, color coding, and illuminated directional signs.

Utilization of Space (Book Storage)

During the early planning stages, endless debates were held with scientists and other "experts" regarding the amount of stacks space which should be provided. Even at that time, many people insisted that by the time the building was completed, the book would be obsolete and the bulk of information now in printed form would be stored in microform or on magnetic tape. Fortunately, this group did not win the argument, and the plans provided for stacks which would accommodate publications for the next 15-20 years. Like the participants at the Educational Facilities Laboratories Seminar, we concluded "that for at least the next 20 years, the book will remain an irreplaceable means of information."

Equally lengthy debates were also held as to whether or not the building should be designed for future expansion through additional floors or wings. After careful consideration of the problem, we concluded that, at least in the Ottawa area, if and when we required more shelf space, it would be cheaper and more effective to obtain the needed accommodation by building or renting warehouse space on the outskirts of the city, rather than attempt to modify the building. Accordingly, the present structure is not designed to be enlarged.

The five stack floors, constructed around a centre core containing public elevators and a lounge-reading area, provide shelving for 2,000,000 volumes. Each floor is identical in size and layout and contains 66,000 linear feet of shelving to accommodate 400,000 volumes - a total of 50 miles of shelving. Except for the main corridors, the shelves are spaced 36 inches apart.

I am convinced that in order to exploit more fully existing information resources and provide new services, we will be seeking additional

staff working space before we require more shelving accommodation. Accordingly, stack floors are designed for easy conversion to office space.
The lighting is excellent, and the 12-foot ceiling height will permit a
drop ceiling installation with a height of 8 feet.

Intra-Building Communication

In a building as large as the one housing CISTI, it is essential to
have equipment which will facilitate communication among the staff and
expedite the flow of material within the building.

To supplement the normal telephone and inter-office lines, we have
installed a UHF combined two-way radio and personal paging system to contact staff within the building, or within a 10-mile radius of the building. The person paged receives both a tone signal and a message. The
radio system provides for direct two-way communication between the driver
of our station wagon, the Building Coordinator, and the Administrative
Assistant.

The entire stack area is served by a talk-back paging system linked
to the main Information Desk.

To cope with the flow of material in the building, the most important piece of equipment is the high-volume vertical and horizontal electronic conveyor system. This system, linking all the stack floors, Interlibrary Loan, Reprography, Bindery, and Supply and Shipping Rooms, provides for the transportation of material in fiberglass containers 20½" x
17" x 10", with a net carrying capacity of 31 lbs. These boxes are
carried at a speed of 8 per minute in the vertical section and 4 per minute in the horizontal section. Because of the high speed of the system
and its ability to handle small items such as call slips and messages going to the stack floors, our decision not to install a pneumatic tube system has been amply justified.

I recall that during our early visits to libraries in the United
States, one piece of advice which was always offered was "be sure and install plenty of conduits to carry various types of cables to all parts of
the building." This advice was taken to heart, and under-floor triducts
carrying power and telephone lines and other communication links have been
installed on all floors. With the ducts spaced every 4½ feet on centres,
and triple pedestal connections every 18 inches, we have a grid which provides access to cables at even the most unpredictable locations.

Inter-Building Communication

In this area of communication, there has been no technical breakthrough which will speed up or simplify communication between CISTI and
other parts of Canada. We must still rely on the postal services, telephone, and Telex or TWX. We have three Telex machines which are used primarily to handle the interlibrary loan traffic.

Facsimile transmission equipment was installed about six years ago,
but contrary to hopes and expectations, it has not in Canada proved to be
a popular means of communication. I gather the same holds true in the
United States. The major constraints to the users of this means of commu-

nication are its relatively slow speed of operation and high costs, particularly over long distances. Within a local calling area, the technique works well, but over long distances, as for example between Ottawa
and Calgary, a distance of some 2,000 miles, where we ran extensive tests,
potential customers were reluctant to pay the $5.60 per page transmitted.

In any case, if and when facsimile transmission becomes, for libraries, a viable means of communication, it will be as a replacement for
shipping photocopies by mail and will have no significant effect on the'
design or layout of library buildings.

Reprography

The CISTI Library, serving as it does not only as the National Science Library of Canada, but also as a National Lending Library, is at present processing up to 600 requests per day for loans or photocopies. Accordingly, provision has been made for two large work areas 62' x 35' (totalling about 2200 sq.ft.) to house a wide variety of photocopying machines, sorters, collators, multilith machine, an electrostatic copier for
production of plates, and related equipment used in the production of our
in-house publications. This area adjoins the Interlibrary Loan offices
and is linked to all stack floors and the Interlibrary Loan area by the
conveyor system.

The development of this reprography area was also a controversial
subject during the early planning stages. We questioned whether a system
should be adopted similar to that at the National Library of Medicine,
where material is copied with cameras located on each stack floor, or
whether the publications should be sent to a central point for copying.
There is not time to discuss the pros and cons of these two alternatives,
suffice to say we adopted the latter. This arrangement works most effectively where publications to be copied are sent to the Reprography
Room by the conveyor. The basket containing the publications goes directly to a copying machine. After copying, the volumes go back into the same
basket which is then returned to its appropriate stack. This procedure reduces to a minimum the amount of time when any publication is off the
shelf.

We have made two concessions to this arrangement: first, for the
convenience of staff and clients, copying machines are located at strategic points throughout the building such as in the Reference Department,
the area housing the abstracting and indexing services, and in such departments as Acquisitions, Circulation, Main Information Desk, and the Administrative Area. Secondly, while still in our old location and in order
to gain shelving space, all journals published prior to 1950 (some 40,000
volumes) were moved to a warehouse, together with a copying machine and
operator. This arrangement was retained after moving to the new building.
These volumes, with a Xerox machine and operator, are located on one stack
floor. Despite studies showing the extent to which the use of publications
drops off after 5-6 years, we find it necessary to have a full-time operator to cope with the number of requests for copies of papers from these
older journals.

This arrangement cuts to a minimum the handling and transportation of
older volumes, many of which are in a bad state of repair. For the browser

or the person who forgets the cutoff date, it may mean going to two different stack floors to consult consecutive volumes of a journal.

Computer and EDP Facilities

Since one of CISTI's major objectives is to be innovative and develop
new techniques to expedite the dissemination or transfer of information,
EDP plays a large role in our day-to-day operations. Accordingly, one
floor in the core area, essentially a stack floor, is designed to house
computer facilities and supporting activities.

This area consists of a computer room of approximately 20,000 sq.ft.,
complete with pedestal flooring, high capacity air conditioning equipment,
automatic opening doors, and a Halon fire-extinguishing system. This is
complemented by an office area of 10,000 sq.ft.

At the present time, the NRC's computer facilities (IBM 360 Model 67
TSS) are able to cope with our data processing requirements. This computer floor is therefore as yet unoccupied.

The triduct grid system which I mentioned earlier enables us to locate computer terminals at any point in the building. Thus, we have terminals located in the Reference Department, the area where CAN/SDI and
CAN/OLE services are maintained, the Health Sciences Resource Centre Section for accessing MEDLINE, and in the Systems Design and Development Section. Portable terminals are used for instructionsl seminars and workshops in the various conference rooms. As required, terminals can be installed in other areas such as the Cataloguing and Acquisitions Department
and in individual carrels located on the stack floors - all for accessing
and inputting data to a central storage bank.

Miscellaneous

Other features which take advantage of various technological developments need only be mentioned briefly.

The main Conference Room, with a seating capacity of 150, can be divided into two rooms, each seating 75. Each room is served by simultaneous
translation equipment supported by audio-amplification and recording devices. All of these facilities can be operated separately, or simultaneously to serve two ongoing meetings. The system is a so-called "unwired"
one where the microphones are plugged into under-table wiring for any configuration and where earsets are unwired and portable.

CISTI is currently receiving approximately 50,000 microfiche per
year and is also developing in cassette or microfiche format, duplicate
sets of the most frequently cited journals. To facilitate the use of this
material, a large area on the second floor is equipped for reader use and
for the storage and processing of the material.

The user reading area has variable intensity lighting. Equipment for
reproducing microfiche or producing hard copy from the fiche is located in
close proximity to the storage area. To further facilitate the use of this
material, inexpensive and portable readers, such as the Kodak Ektolite 120,
are located at strategic points in all staff and public work areas.

The building is noteworthy for the manner in which, through the use of light wells and skylights, daylight enters all public and work areas. This, supported by fluorescent lighting, gives a high level of illumination, higher than Keyes Metcalf would approve. For example, in the Cataloguing and Reference Departments we have an intensity of up to 160-185 foot candles (with sunlight); in the Conference Room, 140-155 foot candles; and in the Stacks and study carrels, 40-55 foot candles. Lighting throughout the building is controlled by means of a master panel located at the Information Desk.

Ralph Shaw once said that our library literature was too full of papers of the type "how we done it good in Podunk Center." If this talk appears to be of that nature, I apologize. My intention has been to describe how one group of relatively inexperienced library building planners attempted to meet some very specific requirements by exploiting as fully as possible technological developments now in existence and those which seemed imminent in the near future.

DISCUSSION

Jerrold Orne: To my astonishment, this is the first time in my long and varied library life I have heard a librarian say that we do not feel the need for expansion space. I'm pleased to hear it, because I've been an apostle of storage for a long, long time. I don't seem to get anywhere, but I think it's inevitable.

Don Davidson: I'd like to ask Dr. Brown if he used any modern, different, or new devices in relationship to the security of the building.

Brown: Yes, security in the building created a great problem because, after the design of the building was pretty well completed, rather belatedly, the fire commissioners got into the act. We had to install a great many extra exits which we had not planned, so the building is equipped with alarms. There is a central alarm system at the commissioner's desk at the main entrance and at the information desk. We had a great deal of trouble when we moved into the building. People didn't take these alarm doors seriously, and the alarm was ringing all the time. The building was designed, particularly the computer floor, for use twenty-four hours a day, and there is a back entrance which is intended for access to this floor. We have a television camera which watches that entrance, with a screen in the commissioner's office. The camera is so good that a person can hold up an identification card, and the commissioner can read what it says. Once the man is identified, he pushes a button on the door, the alarm mechanism is released, and he can open the door and enter. But we really haven't solved the problem; as I say, it created more problems than we anticipated because of these extra doors which were not in the original plans.

Craig Moore (directed to Poole): I have heard it said in more than one
          place recently that sliding-drawer compact storage is not avail-
          able. Last week the Columbia campus of the University of Mis-
          souri took delivery on some $65,000 worth of sliding-drawer e-
          quipment supplied by C. K. Brown Manufacturing. I think it's
          from Milwaukee. I had the experience of meeting Mr. Brown, in
          the middle of last week, and he stood about eight inches from
          my face and described to me the wisdom of this kind of storage.
          So apparently it's still available. I wasn't a party to how it
          was selected, but I know it's available.

Poole: I'm glad to know that. I did allude to Shelf-Co, which is Mr.
          Brown's organization, and I had been led to believe from discus-
          sion with various people that this was not being sold, but ap-
          parently it is. You may not have all heard Harold Roth who in-
          dicated that "Conserva-File" is still being manufactured by Su-
          preme Equipment Company. This, too, I was unaware of. So there
          are lots of things apparently on the market that don't come to
          the attention of all of us. It pays to look around and investi-
          gate the field pretty thoroughly.
               I might just indicate that the new James Madison Memorial
          Building of L. C. is also making extensive use of security meas-
          ures. We have the same television monitoring cameras at each
          entrance as does Mr. Brown in Canada. We also are using perime-
          ter alarms, ultrasonics. All of the locks on doors to restrict-
          ed spaces, such as our computer areas and certain rare book col-
          lections, our restoration workshops and so forth, are card-acti-
          vated locks; expensive, but they do give us, we think, very full
          control. These sorts of things are coming into use more and
          more, especially in a time when vandalism and arson and things of
          that sort, which we used to consider rather unlikely, are in-
          creasing all around the country.

Schneid (directed to Poole and Roth): I fully concur with Mr. Poole's fig-
          ures of 15,000 sq.ft. holding 630,000 volumes - that works out to
          roughly 40 volumes a square foot versus Mr. Roth's figure of
          50,000 sq.ft. for a million volumes and this is all based on com-
          pact shelving.
               One of the things I don't quite agree with is what Mr. Poole
          said about direct access to the compact shelving. I do know of a
          public library, in particular, in the United States where they do
          have it for the public to use; the compact system is working out
          fine.
               On the safety aspect of the compact shelving, the primary
          safety feature, in addition to the waist level and the floor lev-
          el devices, is the button that you push to go into the aisle.
          When that button is pushed, a light turns on; and no other aisle is
          operable within that module.

Poole: I don't know that any comment particularly needs to be made, ex-
          cept that as far as the use of compact shelving, such as I was de-

scribing, the track-type, is concerned, I think this is an individual decision for the librarian. I think many of us would feel that in a heavily used, active collection where open access is desired, compact shelving might not be as suitable as our traditional shelving, but I know as Mr. Schneid points out, it has been used in some places. I think it's an individual decision on the part of the librarian. I think it's also the kind of decision that should be made very carefully.

Roth: You mentioned earlier than there are some disagreements about the total capacity of any area. For instance, when we talk about one million volumes, we're talking about a million volumes now. With the development of miniaturization, the capacity of this area to hold additional volumes is obviously there. We believe that we have approached what has been an attempt to allow for ultimate use up to maybe four or five million volumes, if miniaturization continues to hold. The problem, of course, is the matter of sizing the volumes, the amount of periodicals that are going to be involved; and I was hoping somebody would ask this question: "Is everything going to be in the stack area?" The answer to that is: "No." This is only the storage area that we're talking about; bibliographic and other materials will be on the floor. There are arrangements for at least a quarter of a million volumes set on the floor, and our building consultant made sure that that was in-put in the program.

Orne: We have heard three excellent presentations related to very important buildings where virtually everything that is known up to now in this area of storage has been considered, and many of those discussed. The balance of the program, as I have just glanced at it, comes to the point which is of most interest to me, and I think, may interest many of you even more. This is not the physical possibilities or the technological development at our present time, but some of the philosophical problems which really do determine what we are going to do. We keep talking about access and availability, now here again about security. We've heard about preservation, and Frazer Poole is an expert on that. There are philosophical ideas that we have had for decades that are going to have to change. In my view, the change will be towards coming to a better understanding of what is really needed now, here, and on the spot. In view of the size, the dimensions of the space we talk about so freely, we're going to have to reconsider what we really have to have and what we can supply; that is, how quickly, how completely we can meet a demand at any given moment and what a reasonable time lag is.

As you know, I have been watching library building, primarily academic, for a long time, so I am one sided. I have been convinced for many years that we've got to find some way of rationalizing the size and money demands and requirements with the service requirements; and they are, I think, beginning to come clearer. In some of the remaining sessions of this meeting, there are going to be extensive discussions of regionalization and depositories and other space-at-a-distance, and perhaps there we will come closer to meeting this point.

Regional cooperation, an alternative to running out of space?

INTRODUCTION

Regional cooperation is increasing in all parts of the country. University administrators have increasingly come to view it as a means to reduce growth of campus libraries. The University of California is one institution that is seriously examining this alternative.

Within the University of California system a number of individual libraries were out of space or on the verge of running out of space. To eliminate, or reduce, the need for construction on individual campuses, a new regional library center was contemplated. It was believed that if all the duplicate, low-use titles could be gathered together in one physical, regional facility, new construction for campus libraries would not be necessary. A regional library facility also suggested other benefits.

1. Less expensive warehouse-type facilities could be constructed on inexpensive land of ample size to provide for extensive future expansion.
2. If operations at this regional center were patterned after those of the National Lending Library in England, delivery of material to a requestor would be swift and the need for library collections of unlimited size on each campus would not be necessary.

Initial studies, however, have indicated that, in fact, duplication of low-use materials is minimal. The duplication is primarily high-use materials required for teaching programs on the individual campuses, duplication which will continue to be necessary regardless of an effective delivery system from a regional center. Dr. Swain updates the University's thinking and activities in this area.

The Research Libraries Group has not included plans for a regional physical facility. It stresses cooperative activities in a number of areas, including resource sharing. Dr. Skipper discusses a number of factors which shed light on possible answers to the question: "Is retionalization a false hope for solving library space problems?"

Moderator's Introduction

Bernard Kreissman, University Librarian
                              University of California at Davis

Just a short time ago, about a year, the University of California system was described to me as nine baronies with the resident robber acceding to cooperation only to the extent that the siege outside his doors leaped the moat. Well, of course, this was a bit of an exaggeration, because the system does have many cooperative features but has been working for several years to develop an even stronger cooperative system-wide approach. One of the men involved very deeply in that development is Dr. Donald Swain, Vice Chancellor for Academic Affairs of the University of California at Davis campus. That is, he is Vice Chancellor for Academic Affairs as of this moment. As of three days from now, July 1st, Dr. Donald Swain will become Vice President for Academic Affairs of the University of California. I'm sorry to lose him from the Davis campus, but I am happy to say that he's going to be involved in the developments of the library system.

Regional library planning for northern campuses of the University of California

DONALD C. SWAIN

Vice President for Academic Affairs,
University of California

Regional library planning, like economic analysis or projecting graduate enrollments in the 1970s, is a chancy business. There are essentially no ground rules - only an increasingly urgent understanding that universities cannot continue to plan and manage libraries as they did in the 1960s. The colorful acronyms coined by various regional planning projects and consortia - from FAUL to CLASS - are enough, if nothing else, to arouse the interest of librarians and academic administrators around the country and to indicate the rhetorical inventiveness and optimism of the people involved. In this kind of planning, one learns by doing.

It is unmistakably clear that we have, like it or not, entered the age of large-scale regional library planning. This is certainly true in California where the sprawling geographic configuration, inflation, space shortages, and continuing budgetary constraints provide fertile ground for such planning. The University of California has recently committed itself to a systemwide approach to library planning, assuming a single university collection rather than nine separate campus collections. The California State University and Colleges system has already implemented centralized planning for its 19 libraries. And, the California State Librarian is attempting to establish a statewide library network that will incorporate not only the UC and CSUC libraries but also the county public libraries of the state.

I decided that perhaps the most useful thing to do would be to present an interpretive summary of a small part of this larger pattern of library planning in California - namely, the efforts of the northern campuses of the University of California (Davis, Berkeley, and Santa Cruz) to plan a regional library system. These efforts, which are still in progress, predated the movement toward unified library planning for the entire U.C. system, and have since been subsumed under that larger umbrella. I should note that my remarks constitute a personal interpreta-

tion and are not in any sense an official summary. As an historian as
well as an administrator, I find it fascinating to be involved in this
rapidly unfolding pattern of change, and I want to take this opportunity
to share with you some of my idiosyncratic impressions.

It was shortage of space that originally impelled us into action.
By 1973, the Berkeley library already found it necessary to transfer a
volume from the main library to storage for every new book added to the
collection. The library at Davis, though not yet as cramped as Berkeley's,
was rapidly running out of space and anticipating the need for storage in
the near future. The two libraries are located about 70 miles apart. Why
not consolidate the planning of storage facilities that would allow us to
maximize efficiency and promote shared use?

The fact that, to some extent, we already drew upon each other's resources was a second factor that brought us into an informal regional library planning alliance. A daily bus linked Davis and Berkeley. Materials increasingly flowed both ways, i.e., from the Davis library to the
Berkeley library as well as from Berkeley to Davis. A daily bus also ran
between Santa Cruz and Berkeley. Could we not try to establish 24- to 48-
hour turnaround times for the exchange of materials among the three campuses, using direct borrowing rather than interlibrary loan procedures?
The Santa Cruz campus at this point joined our informal discussions and
became an enthusiastic partner in our regional planning efforts.

A third factor, by far the most complex, served to encourage us into
a regional planning mode. This was the need to assure that each library
got the most out of its limited space and book acquisition funds. Moving
toward greater cooperation in acquisitions, toward collaboration in deciding which serials to discontinue as budgets got tighter, and toward
the elusive goal, frequently mentioned in Sacramento, of reducing alleged
duplication of holdings, not to mention also toward the prospect of coordinated space use, all seemed to require a regional response.

Swallowing hard, at least in deference to the third factor, the
three campuses set up a task force, composed of the academic Vice Chancellor and University Librarian from each campus, to begin planning on a regional basis. It was anticipated that Stanford University would soon be
invited to join in this regional planning. This has subsequently been
done and Stanford is now participating in the discussions.

Our first task was to agree on certain fundamental planning assumptions. The discussions were hardnosed and tough. After perhaps a half-
dozen meetings, the task force reached consensus. Though many nuances
were discussed, the following main planning assumptions emerged:

1. A regional approach to the library holdings, services, and fa-
    cilities should serve the vital interests of the participating
    campuses and the entire University library system.
2. Regional library planning should be viewed as an extension of
    academic planning and must serve the needs of the instructional
    and research programs of the participating campuses.
3. Methods of governance and administrative arrangements for the
    regional library system should be mutually acceptable to all
    participating campuses as well as to the President of the Uni-
    versity.

4. The regional library system should include, as a minimum, the holdings of Berkeley, Davis, and Santa Cruz libraries. At an early date, private universities, campuses of the CSUC system, and other private libraries, as appropriate, should be invited to participate in the regional system.

5. The regional library system should be conceived as a unified system rather than as several separately defined campus collections. In the long run, the regional collection, which is the sum total of the campus collections, should contain materials developed and maintained on a shared basis. For example, only one copy of certain serials and monographs should be acquired if that number is sufficient to serve the needs of the region.

6. As stored materials increase in volume, coordinated handling of storage should be undertaken so as to encourage ready access, on a regional basis, to all stored materials.

7. The greatest possible reliance on intercampus cooperation and resource sharing should be a central consideration in planning for the regional system. Certain library functions, to be carefully defined, should be performed on a regional basis to facilitate coordination of purchases (or discontinuation) of serials, expensive sets and monographs, foreign language dissertations, rare books, etc.

8. Highest priority should be placed on the development of bibliographic access to the holdings of the regional system. The objective should be to enable any user on any participating campus to have ready access to all holdings in the regional system.

9. A direct borrowing system should be established to enable users on various campuses in the regional system to borrow directly and quickly from each of the libraries in the system.

10. If a centralized library facility (i.e., new space) is eventually needed, its location is to be determined on the basis of thorough consultation among the participating campuses of the President's Office. Meanwhile, the question of location should remain open and undecided.

The task force in its first two years commissioned specific staff projects, some of a highly technical nature, to provide additional planning information. For example: a study of the overlap in serials holdings among the participating libraries, testing various definitions of "low-use;" a study of monographs and the dimensions of possible overlap in this category of holdings; a study of the different forms of governance used in other regional systems; a close examination of intercampus loan procedures and possible ways of facilitating direct intercampus borrowing; an exploration of the possibility of uniform lending policies at all campuses. Most of these staff projects are still under way, but we assume this information will provide the foundation for the specific decisions that must be made as we begin implementing our plans.

University-wide decisions to explore the possibility of a tie-in with BALLOTS and to establish pilot programs in automated circulation systems, have moved us along more quickly in these two areas than would have been possible by working strictly within the regional framework.

Looking back over the two years or so that have elapsed since this project began, I want to note five general "lessons" that have grown out of our experience.

1. First, the notion that centralized regional storage facilities would be necessary, which was one of the ideas we began with and that brought us together, evolved from a central planning assumption to a peripheral assumption. As we thought about various options, it gradually emerged that we might not need centralized regional storage space. We agreed that the question should remain open to discussion in the future, but we preferred, in the beginning, to conceptualize a regional collection to be housed on the campuses. Storage would be coordinated so that all little-used materials in one particular field would be sent to one campus; all little-used materials in another field would be sent to another campus, and so on. Decentralized storage space, which would be considerably less expensive to construct than regular library space, would be planned on each campus as library facilities expanded. Thus users who wanted to draw on the stored materials could utilize the improved direct intercampus borrowing system that was planned, and questions of centralized staffing and acquisitions could be postponed for a while. The development of a central regional library facility that would grow by incremental stages into a substantial research library in its own right was not abandoned. But it is now on the back burner and will depend on careful cost benefit analysis in the future. It is obvious, in the meantime, that the development of a regional system will not entirely obviate the need for additional library space on the campuses. We hope the rate of expansion can be slowed down.

2. A second lesson emerged. Regional library planning is no panacea for the difficult problems of library financing and space shortages in the 1970s. Regional planning is likely in the short run to increase, not decrease, total library costs because of the need for automated bibliographic access, circulation control mechanisms, and new regional facilities. But the efficiency of the library system will be considerably increased and the university and the state will be assured that scarce resources are in fact being maximized and used efficiently. In the long run, library service will be improved because the larger regional holdings, organized effectively as a single collection, with direct borrowing rather than interlibrary loan, is a significantly richer collection than any single library in the system.

3. A third lesson: the faculty, though cautious and a little skeptical, have gone along with regional library planning. The notion that the Davis library, for example, must "own" and retain all the volumes it acquires is dying; and the comforting knowledge that certain volumes are in the stacks in the campus library will become less and less important as the capability to get volumes quickly to users, regardless of location, is developed. Academic Senate committees have been kept informed and have agreed to the proposed regional system - at least so far - and have taken a rather farsighted view of the need to change some of the assumptions underlying library planning. This point is hard to exaggerate. In our ex-

perience, other groups, including some librarians who may fear automation or may have ego involvement in accumulating more and more books in their own libraries, may prove to be more recalcitrant.

4.   A fourth lesson, a very important one, is that regional library planning tends to encourage intercampus cooperation generally. Once started, cooperation can be quite contagious. For example, having heard about the efforts at the policy level to move toward regionalization, the government document librarians from Davis, Berkeley, and Santa Cruz decided on their own to get together to coordinate their activities. This spin-off effect, which came as a bonus, augurs well for the future of regional cooperation.

5.   The fifth and last lesson I want to point out is that in regional library planning, policy-making should not be left to librarians alone. Basic institutional policies are at stake which require high-level administrative participation. Moreover librarians, like other human beings, have been known to be content with the status quo. Outside administrators, though perhaps unfamiliar with the technical details of library management, can sometimes raise issues that librarians themselves are reluctant to raise, and they can place library planning in a wider institutional framework. The librarians in turn can save the outside administrators from egregious technical errors. Above all, people like Vice Chancellors can help the librarians take the heat that is inevitably generated as regional planning becomes an implemented reality. Close working relations are indispensable between chief librarians and campuswide or systemwide administrators.

I would not want to exaggerate the progress we have made in the past two years. The pace has been slow and at times tedious. Many pitfalls remain. The proverbial thousand-mile journey begins, of course, with a single step. The three northern campuses of the University of California have taken that first step gingerly. Other steps will follow, and I am confident they will be less gingerly taken.

The Research Libraries Group and the library space problem

JAMES SKIPPER

Director, Research Libraries Group

The Research Libraries Group is comprised of the libraries of Columbia, Harvard, and Yale Universities and the Research Libraries of the New York Public Library. The organization was formed to improve library services to the users of the four institutions and to increase the efficiency of their operations. These libraries are seeking answers similar to the dynamics of the potted plant - or how to remain healthy and vigorous while being hostage to limited growth. As our members, representing some of the largest research collections available, recognize that they can no longer attempt local self-sufficiency in providing services or collections for their constituents, RLG is being developed as a viable alternative to attempted self-sufficiency.

It has occurred to me that, from the standpoint of gallows humor, the massive loss in purchasing power over recent years due to inflation, the devaluation of the dollar abroad, and general levelling of funding support from local, state, and federal authorities will, in itself, make a substantial contribution to solving our space problems.

In implementing its major objectives, RLG has presently three programs, chosen to focus available resources and energies on a very limited number of interrelated objectives.

First, we have developed a Shared Access Program to afford quicker and more dependable access to the combined pool of over 26.5 million volumes in our collections. Secondly, we are in the process of establishing several related programs to reduce unnecessary duplication in the future development of our collections. Our third effort is to design and construct a single, computer-based bibliographic processing system to serve the needs of member libraries. I should mention that it is our intention to invite other libraries to participate in RLG programs at the appropriate time.

Like any library or group of libraries which collects comprehensively in support of teaching and research, RLG members are concerned with space problems. Each of our libraries, with net accessions ranging from 80,000 to 170,000 volumes per year, must find an average of approximately two to three linear miles of shelving to accommodate each year's acquisitions. As each member is part of a private institution, capital funds for construction and endowment for building maintenance and utilities must be solicited in a presently depressed economic market. It has been estimated that for privately supported libraries approximately $200 per square foot is required to cover costs.

Much before the advent of RLG, its members were developing their own solutions to the space problem. These solutions range from the founding of the New England Deposit Library by Harvard - which is simply rental space available to libraries, to the compact shelving program at Yale which attracted much attention a decade or more ago. The Yale program involved conventional shelving with narrow aisles and perhaps ten shelves per section (rather than seven), made possible by shelving books on their fore-edge. The New York Public Library Research Libraries, finding it impossible to expand their site on the corner of Fifth Avenue and 42nd Street, acquired a warehouse for their newspapers and other collections. Columbia, like many libraries, has developed a musical chairs approach to storage by providing temporary accommodations in new libraries or other buildings on campus, with shifting being required as the original tenant demands the space.

Fifteen or twenty years ago, there was discussion of creating a warehouse for little-used collections at some point geographically central to NYPL, Columbia, Yale, and other university libraries in New England. Nothing came of the idea at the time - largely because libraries then were still committed to attempting local self-sufficiency in providing services to their constituents. Institutions at that time were as reluctant to share libraries as they would have been to share football teams. Institutional pride was - and still is - a powerful force. However, today, either as a result of maturity, or desperation born of economic distress, we are seeing the development of library consortia as organizational responses to existing difficulties. Consortia are, of course, nothing new and RLG is a relative late-comer to this development. However, RLG is unique and significant considering the character of the institutions involved and the depth of commitment which has been made by the directors of these libraries.

It can be argued that if cooperative efforts continue to grow among libraries, the potential effect of consortia in helping to resolve the space problem would be increased in several respects. First, through cooperative action libraries might agree to store lesser-used materials or collections jointly, and thus achieve space economies by disposing of titles which are duplicated. As you know, the great bulk of research collections falls within the "lesser-used" category. However, before we become too sanguine about this prospect for reducing space needs, we should be fully aware of the cost elements involved in adopting various options. These costs fall upon either the library - or the user - and sometimes both.

In designing an ideal system for housing books, it can be argued that those volumes identified as being relatively lesser-used should be transferred to storage. This procedure should produce the least interference with user access to the most active segment of the collection. This approach is both difficult and expensive to implement. The selection process involving a volume-by-volume analysis can be very costly, especially when review by more than one individual is required. Even more expensive is the operation of modifying catalog records to indicate transfers or withdrawals. In many instances these costs exceed the value of the space saved and involve sums which are not available to libraries today.

There are, of course, shortcuts which can be used to reduce expenditures, but these usually result in nothing more than transferring the cost to the user. The user "pays" when storage locations are not indicated in the public card catalog, many libraries having omitted changes in public records to save costs. Block transfers or storing sections of collections may reduce selection and record maintenance costs, but again the reader pays through the inconvenience of actively used titles being unavailable, and his inability to browse in the storage collection is a disadvantage. Lack of "browsability" involves unmeasurable costs in frustrated serendipity and inefficiency as indexes and tables of contents cannot be examined in lieu of secondary bibliographic access. Delivery systems for stored items may involve a range in efficiency and related costs, and again, the lesser cost can usually be associated with greater inconvenience to the user.

The user should also be considered when examining alternatives such as microfilm. What is the relative threshold of inconvenience for the reader in using various formats of microforms as surrogates for different types of text? What are the real "savings" when space and the expense of reading machines, coupled with reduced use of surrogate over original text, are calculated?

In summary, I am convinced that good arguments can be made to the effect that if the user is not to assume an unconscionable burden of the costs, decentralized storage may not be economically justified.

As we all know, however, economic justification and concerns for reader welfare must sometimes be tempered by the absolute absence of space to expand existing library facilities, and decentralized storage of some type becomes the only available solution.

Consortia might also be said to have the potential for reducing space needs by eliminating unnecessary duplication in the development of future collections. This may be, although within RLG I doubt that this type of program will have much effect. It is true that we intend to examine seriously future duplication among our collections, but it is anticipated that the savings will be used in acquiring additional unique titles, rather than resulting in the purchase of a lesser total number of books. For some reason there are those in the publishing community, especially in New York, who seem to find this concept very difficult to understand.

Beyond book collections - which occupy perhaps 25%-35% of the square footage in academic library buildings - what about the balance of the space as related to seating readers and providing work space for staff? It is difficult to make projections for individual institutions, much less attempting to divine the effect of cooperative action on space needs for people. However, it is certain that within the research library community, at least, we will not be doubling our staffs as we did in the 1960s. As consortia become more involved with mechanization, individual libraries will be able to provide better, and less expensive, bibliographic control which should facilitate not only greater storage efficiency, but also afford some space savings due to better utilization of library staff by the avoidance of continuing the maintenance of large files by manual methods.

As I was not able to attend earlier sessions of this conference, I do not know whether the topic of demand publication was related to library space requirements. This, of course, has little to do with RLG or consortia as such - but it is possible that the concept may have something to do with future space requirements in libraries - or bookstores, for that matter. I refer to the process of transmitting scholarly information from the conceptual pen of the investigator to the consciousness of the reader. Society has developed a number of mechanisms to accomplish this purpose, some of which are yet to be fully understood. For the past several hundred years the printing press in its various configurations has been central to the publication of scholarly information. The journal format was developed in the 17th century to increase the speed and regularity of information dissemination, and with post-World War II scientific developments the technical report was developed as a new form to avoid delays in journal publication. Ancillary activities have involved the quality controls imposed by journal editors and reviewers, and bibliographic access has been provided with varying degrees of success by abstracting and indexing publications.

However, the dissemination of information is still a rather unselective process. It is well recognized that the average reader wants only a small fraction of the information contained in a journal issue or a monograph. Why should he or she have to purchase or subscribe to unwanted information? The question is whether the economics and technology of information transfer can be coupled with electronic and optical techniques which will allow the process to be more sharply focused on identifying and providing only the information wanted by an individual. If this can happen, will libraries modify their function of being local repositories of information and adopt the role of providing access services to data not in their own collections, but in data bases miles away? This is already happening in indexing control. It may happen in the dissemination of text, with some interesting implications for future library space needs.

DISCUSSION

Pat Sachs: Granting the magnitude of the growth problems for university libraries and the needs of the clientele for, on occasion, almost everything in print, I would appreciate some comment from the panelists concerning their wisdom relating to the growth of undergraduate collections for undergraduate colleges. I think I am one of those persons who is beginning to question, together with some of my colleagues from undergraduate colleges, such as Daniel Gore, whether or not undergraduate college collections should indeed continue to grow or whether at some point you can establish something like an optimal size related to the enrollment of the college. Of course, together with that is the auxiliary problem of what does the undergraduate college do then in making some demands on its big brothers, the universities, for supplying them with some occasional needs? Certainly some type of compensation system would have to be established if indeed such a relationship is desirable. Then, of course, there's a very practical problem of what do you do at home when the size of the collection and the growth of the collection have always been taken by the institution as part of its identity related to the total strength of its educational institution. We run into the problems of having our collection size compared with the collection size of Amherst or Mount Holyoke or the other prestigious undergraduate colleges; and, of course, there is a great deal of reluctance on the part of the administration and the faculty to consider any sort of containment policy for the growth of the undergraduate collection.

Skipper: You raised some significant questions, most of which are interrelated. First of all, I assume we accept the definition of an undergraduate collection supporting only the teaching activity, not the research activity. We start with that premise. The number of books - of course, the absolute number of books - I don't think anyone can describe. There have been formulae. We have experience. We can point to institutions which we consider to be those of excellence. They have collections of a certain size, so a lot of libraries try to emulate the size of those particular collections. The number of courses being taught, the curriculum, the structure of the curriculum, and, to a lesser extent, student population have a direct effect on the desirable number of books.

I'd like to make the point that's frequently overlooked, that in a college library you need approximately the same number of books to support a given curriculum regardless of whether you have one hundred or one thousand students using that collection. The number of multiple copies you have on course reserve, of course, is a direct reflection of student population, but the number of books it takes to support a teaching program is not as dependent on student population. My personal view is that the undergraduate collection should be a revolving collection with items which are not used coming out of that collection, new items going into it. This is not an absolute steady state, but it certainly does suggest that the growth rate of an undergraduate collection is substantially different, or should be substantially different, from that which characterizes the research library.

What can college collections expect when demands on their collections go beyond their present competence? Faculties in colleges want to continue to write and do research, and yet the structure of that library is not designed to accommodate the needs, the undergraduate teaching needs, of neighboring colleges, because of the type of material wanted, which is characterized by high density use, usually current publication. In my opinion, it is the responsibility of the college itself to supply books needed by their own students. There are, however, peripheral materials such as United Nations documents; and occasionally a student

writing an honor paper may have to have access to to this type
of specialized material. If it can be limited to the exceptional, lesser-used type of material in the research library,
then there is chance for accommodation. If the demand is
steady, then there should certainly be some type of financial
contribution.

I made a very rough calculation with the Research Libraries Group, and I found that they requested about 8,000 volumes
from outside their group each year from other institutions.
They lent about 110,000 volumes to other institutions. In
other words, they had a trade balance of approximately 100,000
volumes. If you assume, as the Westat Research, Inc., study
for the Association of Research Libraries did, that an average
transaction, a completed transaction on interlibrary loans,
costs perhaps $7, this means that those four institutions are
having to set aside approximately $11 million at 6% interest
to take care of this trade deficit in supplying other institutions with material from their collections. So it is very
much a serious problem if it is not controlled and regulated.

Swain: Some of our tentative studies have indicated that in our relations with neighboring colleges, junior colleges and state
colleges in California, the high-demand books that they request
are almost invariably the same high-demand books that we're using on our own campus. Therefore, it doesn't work very well
for our campus to try to provide that service to those other
libraries.

I think, however, that another point needs to be made that
Dr. Skipper didn't make that occurs to me. How an undergraduate library is used is a crucial point; that is, the style of
teaching that is involved. I have a feeling that nationwide
there is a tendency in the direction of doing the kind of undergraduate teaching these days that five to ten years ago was more
like the graduate-level teaching, and this requires greater library use. It requires more of the inquiry method; it requires
more research and rather less lecturing. That kind of trend is,
I think, apparent in many institutions across the country. If
that is true, that puts a larger burden on the undergrauage library, rather resembling the kind of burden that is usual at a
graduate library or a research library. Of course, the size of
the collection doesn't have to be as large, but my point is that
it must accommodate the kinds of teaching styles that the faculty are in fact using.

Kerwin (directed to Swain): You stated that library planning is an extension of academic planning. My impression, when we talk about
fiefdoms and moats, is that in California, as it is with most
places, there hasn't been a great deal of cooperation on the academic planning. Maybe I'm misinterpreting. If, indeed, the librarians would seem to be out in front of the rest of the academic community, am I to interpret your remark about some hard-nosed
bargaining, being bargaining between the academic officers that

were present rather than librarians, concerning academic planning rather than library planning?

Swain: I am happy to say that that really wasn't the case. The hard-nosed bargaining to which I was referring was going on between campuses. That is, the Davis campus was making sure that the underlying planning assumptions that we were agreeing to would be acceptable to the Davis campus; the Berkeley campus was doing the same thing; Santa Cruz was doing the same thing. It took some hard-nosed bargaining, but we did eventually work out a large area of agreement. That's what I was referring to.

As for academic planning, in California we do have a certain compulsion for academic planning. I wouldn't contend that it's all effective, but we do have a lot of it. The Governor makes various characterizations of our planning efforts; most recently he called our academic plan within the university "squid-like" in allusion to all the ink being put out just to obscure rather than to clarify anything. That did strike a responsive chord in certain audiences, including some within the university. But we do have a strong and very comprehensive effort under way to do academic planning in the University of California, and I think that that is going to become more and more important in the future. For that reason, it seems to me, library planning must fit into that larger scheme; and that is what's happening, I believe, in California.

Kreissman: I believe a more direct answer is in relation to a system of curricula. Am I correct in assuming that that was the base? Now to be very honest about it, this has not surfaced to any large degree among the group that Dr. Swain was referring to. However, I am happy to say that from the faculty itself, from the faculty senate, a major document is now under review to explore exactly what you had in mind. I think the librarians once again will be behind such an effort to develop planning as an academic operation and which the library then rightfully follows rather than tries to take the brunt of an operation, which is normally to be held by and borne by the academic officers and the academic administrators.

Metcalf: I'm going to make a number of very wicked comments. Now, first comes the question of duplication. When I went to Harvard, I was told Harvard never duplicated books. Of course, we were very much decentralized and there was tremendous duplication between libraries, but we didn't duplicate reserve books. The result was students, undergraduates, couldn't get the books that they were asked to read. This was many years ago when you could buy more books for a smaller amount of money than you can today. We added $10,000 a year to our reserve book account and were able to cut the staff by $12,000 because we didn't spend their time chasing their tails around the room.

Second, I regret the present financial situation in libraries

very much, but if it would just get over quickly, I think it
would do us a good deal of good. It's going to add to our cooperation. Twenty years ago a large share of the librarians in
this country were empire builders. They would try and provide
a bigger library than their neighbors, whether they needed to
do so or not.

Now, I am even going to criticize college presidents.
College presidents did the same thing. I remember dealing with
a college president who was starting a new graduate school. It
wasn't needed at the time; there was a surplus of graduates of
that type of graduate school in the country. He said, "It'll
give me more graduate school subjects than any other college in
the country, and I'm going to do it." I know that college presidents year after year accepted gifts, particularly the private
universities, of professorships in subjects where there was no
need of it.

Librarians were just as bad. Forty years ago, three of the
great libraries of the country acquired great Frisian collections. There wasn't a single graduate student studying Frisian
in the United States. During the same period, three libraries
began to collect intensively Icelandic books. There were at
that particular time no Icelandic students. Harvard was persuaded many years ago by a vote of the corporation that it
would never start or accept a gift for a new professorship without considering the library implications. When an offer came
for $1 million to start a new Egyptology collection, it was turn-
ed down because on the average there was only one graduate student in Egyptology in the country each year; and there were other
institutions that had better collections than Harvard in the
field.

We've come a long way in the last 40 years, and I hope we'll
go still farther. The college presidents, chancellors, and the
librarians have got to stop being empire builders. The most encouraging thing about the library situation in the United States
is that today we're becoming more cooperative, and I hope it can
continue.

Rift: I would like to speak to the question of the size of college collections. I would say that there is no more reason to limit the
size of college collections than there is reason to limit any
other collection. We must have access wherever we are, and it
is connected only with the possibility of obtaining that material
in some other cooperative way. I would further state that there
is a difference, even if the program is exactly the same in two
colleges. If the student body is larger with relatively un-
structured studies, the demand for different material is very
much related to the student size.

Mr. Swain made the remark that today in undergraduate colleges many studies are undertaken with the intensity of graduate
studies. That is even more true today because the students, the
undergraduate students, work directly with the professors, and

they are taking courses with graduate students in many of the prestigious universities. Therefore, the demands are much larger.

Now, the pattern of lending that Mr. Skipper mentioned is not typical in other regions. I know in my region of up-state New York there is just as much borrowing going on between undergraduate colleges as there is between universities and colleges. It depends very much on the size of the collection; the larger the collection the more borrowing there is. If you have larger universities, there is more borrowing from them. In fact, in our situation in which we are next to a prestigious university, we are finding that the undergraduate students from that university are coming to our college because access to much of the intermediate material that is not in their undergraduate library is much easier than in their graduate library.

Finally, I would like to state that when you get to the level of the California cooperative venture, then where the material is located is not any more dependent on the academic program; especially if we are talking about bringing in other institutions, not just the university.

Skipper: I would like to comment on the last two remarks made. I carefully avoided suggesting any absolute number of books or volumes which would be desirable for an undergraduate collection, because obviously this number depends on the way you teach school.

I did a consulting job at St. John's College in Annapolis, Maryland, about ten years ago, and I was amazed at the small number of books in that library and the small number of books they anticipated adding to that collection. This, of course, influenced the kind of building that I was asked to consult with them on, a new library building. As you know, at St. John's they teach from the Great Books curriculum, an intensive reading of, perhaps, one hundred books with very little investigative work going on on the part of the students.

On the other hand, if you have a curriculum that involves a great deal of investigative work, paper writing, things of this type, you do need a larger number of volumes in your collection. I certainly do not subscribe to the fact that an undergraduate collection can be finite in meeting the needs of its students. You do have to go beyond any particular undergraduate collection. I recall at Berkeley the figures were roughly 25% of the circulation from the research collection for undergraduates, and this was after the installation of a superb undergraduate library and a collection of 60,000 to 80,000 books. This goes on at other schools as well. I think one of the solutions to this, to pick an example, would be the NYSILL approach in New York State where they do have a network; and requests are referred on a hierarchical basis; and monies are paid for services for providing this type of service and lending books which are not available in their local collections.

Now a word about curriculum and the attitude of the faculty

toward all of this. It's obvious that libraries are in the business of supporting teaching and research programs. As Keyes Metcalf has said, if some ambitious president starts a program in Mongolian studies, it falls to the library to attempt to scramble around and find the money to buy the books to support that particular program. Our attitude in RLG is to initially maintain a very low profile as far as talking to faculties directly about consolidating courses in Albanian or Icelandic studies or any of these esoteric areas. First of all, we want to establish our credibility, the fact that we can deliver speedily and dependably from this pool of materials within the four libraries. We have established a Telex network; we have contracts with United Parcel. We have a bibliographic center in space provided by Yale University to monitor this traffic and to maintain supporting programs for the shared access program. We intend to bring into our board of directors the top academic officer from each of the four institutions, so that they will be exposed to the problems we have, the ways in which we are going to set about to solve those problems, on a cooperative basis. Hopefully, if the expectations that cooperation is indeed contagious are fulfilled, some of this will spill over into the area of course and curriculum development, which in itself is a very sticky bit of business. Again, at Berkeley, I was on the course and curriculum committee; and the politics of this situation, as most of you know, is just unreal.

The last point I'd like to make, as far as RLG is concerned, is that we admit that the practical operational problems of mounting our programs are very difficult. These are four old, complex institutions, and it's very difficult to design systems which accommodate the needs and the expectations of each of them. But my constant sermon in talking with staff of these libraries and with their faculties is that the mechanical problems, serious as they are, the policy problems, serious as they are, are very minor compared to our major objective which is to change the attitude and perception on the part of the faculties and library staffs concerning access to collections. Because at the present time, or at least in the recent past, your average librarian, your average faculty member got their sense of professional satisfaction, their sense of institutional pride, from a set of quantitative statistics: how big is your budget? how big is your collection? how fast is it growing? how many seats do you have? how big is your building? and so forth. We have to change that attitude so that professional satisfaction and pride comes from being able to serve your constituent, regardless of where that book is located. You couldn't care less where your electricity is generated; it's here for you to use. This is the attitude that we hope to develop among the constituent library staffs and faculties of the Research Library Group.

Kreissman: I do know that the library world is looking to RLG, because we know that what happens at RLG is going to have a spill-over effect of tremendous proportions throughout the library world. I think I can say the same thing in relation to the California system development. Here, too, the models that develop will probably have influence and impact far beyond the confines of the borders of California.

New building,
library addition, or
renovation?

INTRODUCTION

Alternatives to the library space problem are being explored on many fronts. After this preconference was deep into the planning stage, a notice was received announcing the "Associated Colleges of the Midwest Conference on Space, Growth, and Performance Problems of College and University Libraries." The papers presented were intended to survey the current space problems of academic libraries, and present break-through strategies to reduce collection size, curb collection growth, improve delivery of wanted publications, eliminate the need for new construction. But all library space problems cannot be resolved by such changes in operating procedures nor by utilization of new types of equipment and of new technologies. Renovation of existing building space or construction of new space is often the only solution that will realistically suffice to satisfy a library's functional requirements.

Keyes Metcalf expressed skepticism that the renovation alternative alone could resolve serious space problems. Renovation together with the addition of new space is a more likely alternative for an existing library. Renovation presents its own set of problems emanating from serious disruption of on-going library activity with the inevitable noise and dirt accompanying construction. Conversion of an existing non-library building for library use is another alternative that is especially attractive in an era of conservation of resources; however, this issue was not addressed in this preconference.

The University of British Columbia was of particular interest, because its alternative was to build an underground facility for its undergraduate library. The University of California's experience with reception to the idea of an underground addition ranged from state officials' concern that building costs would be higher than for a structure on ground to the concern of some staff and faculty who could only view windowless space as anathema to the desired human condition. For conservationists, a below-ground structure preserves open space and provides the potential for

conserving energy. All of these factors have not been dealt with in depth
in these proceedings, but they merit further study; and below-ground construction deserves serious consideration as a building alternative.

Renovations and additions are not always cost effective nor is it
always possible to correct building problems by utilizing these alternatives. Often a new building is the only viable solution. Nancy
McAdams describes this type of situation at the University of Texas.
When all other alternatives to running out of space have been utilized or
analyzed and proved to be ineffective, then new construction is the alternative that librarians must convince the funding bodies to support. This
is a difficult task in the 1970s.

Problems of renovating an existing library building

KEYES METCALF
Library Building Consultant

I heartily believe in renovation, although I confess it isn't going to solve all of our problems and it presents at least eleven problems that I will discuss to make certain that you pay attention to them before you go into extensive renovation. Many of you attended the building planning sessions in New York a year ago. The one entitled "Renovation - Budget Crisis/Energy Crisis" had three speakers - an imaginative architect, a great consulting engineer, and an illumination expert (Walter Netsch of Skidmore, Owings, and Merrill; Fred Dubin; and Richard Kelly, respectively). You will find that my talk today while covering the same subject will be quite different, because it is written from a librarian's point of view and will take only 20 minutes instead of the hour and a half taken by the three speakers together. I shall, however, emphasize the present financial situation as was done last year.

All buildings sooner or later need renovation, such as repainting or new floor covering. But libraries tend more than most other structures to increase their space requirements and on the average, they double their space requirements every 16 or 18 years, something which Fremont Rider found years ago and which has been confirmed by many others. This has been going on for well over two hundred years. We hope that it is not going to continue to go on at that rate, but I can assure you we are not going to run into the trouble that Dean Hudnut spoke of thirty years ago. Therefore, renovation alone is generally insufficient.

Full renovation of an old building if often desirable only at the same time an addition is provided. Sometimes an addition is impossible or unwise due to site and other problems; and a completely new building should be the solution to the space problem, particularly if the present building can be used to advantage for other purposes. I confess that it is often impossible to get a new building.

Whether an addition or only a renovation is decided upon, the following eleven points should be considered.

Building Program - A program outlining your needs should be pre-pared by a competent person, sometimes the librarian, sometimes someone even more competent, to serve three distinct purposes:

1. To make you, as the librarian, think carefully about your needs and priorities.
2. To enable your library committee and others concerned to think carefully about these needs and priorities and to give you backing.
3. To tell the architect what you want him to provide.

Gaining Space in an Existing Building - Unless your present building is not now used to advantage, it will be difficult to add to its capacity for readers, books, and staff, or new facilities of any kind. There are, however, four ways of gaining space in an old building:

1. Rearrange space assignments so as to use it to better advantage.
2. Install compact shelving in places which will hold the addition-al load. Too often compact shelving costs more than the same square footage that could be made available in an addition with standard stacks, but as space costs increase, this may not con-tinue to be the case.
3. Replace regular books and other materials with micro-reproduc-tions.
4. Decentralize, as Bob Walsh told us has been going on at Harvard for generations.

Overcrowding - Make sure in any renovation that available space is used to advantage, but do not crowd seating, staff, or bookstacks so as to discourage readers or handicap the staff. I have seen too many cases where, to gain space, additions of that kind have been made - more tables, crowding more staff in limited space, and handicapping the ser-vices of the library.

The Site - Before attempting extensive and expensive renovation, make sure that the site permits an addition that will be satisfactory functionally and aesthetically later when space gives out, as it prob-ably will if past experience repeats itself.

Mechanical System - Satisfactory renovation may include a new heat-ing and ventilation system and air conditioning. Libraries should be air conditioned not just for the comfort of the staff but, of greater importance, for the preservation of the collections, particularly if they include difficult-to-replace books. Remember that it is more ex-pensive to install air conditioning in an old building than in a new construction, and sometimes it is practically impossible.

Lighting - It is often difficult to shift from incandescent to flu-orescent lighting without harming the building aesthetically, but fluo-rescent tubes provide up to three times as much intensity with less heat from the same amount of wattage. Conduit may not have to be changed for the conversion from incandescent to fluorescent lighting at satisfactory light levels even though the building may have previously been under-lighted. Today's power shortage provides a good argument for fluorescent tubes. Most libraries are using more light than needed, and some specialists are more concerned with over-lighting than under-lighting.

The greatest library lighting problem today with our relatively low ceilings is to provide satisfactory quality for work surfaces and for the lower shelves without over-lighting. Shadows and too much contrast and glare become troublesome as intensity is increased. Four-foot squares of ceiling lights, separated by six feet in each direction, leave blind spots and shadows wherever there are bookstacks and carrel partitions. Properly spaced strip lighting with 40-watt, slim-line, 8-foot-long tubes installed in fixtures with good reflectors can eliminate these problems. In a room with a ceiling at least 8'6" high, fixtures should be mounted three to four feet on center. In bookstacks with the same ceiling height, light strips four to six feet on center, mounted at right angles to the stack ranges, use less power and provide satisfactory lighting at a quarter of the cost of what is being done today in our new libraries. It will provide three times as much light as we were using in our libraries in the 1930s. The best ophthalmologists that I know tell me there is much more danger with too much light than not enough. Underlighting may give you a headache but will give you no permanent damage; overlighting may permanently damage your eyes. Keep this in mind if you install new lighting in an old building. Individual carrel or table lights may be troublesome today because of student vandalism and they are not always satisfactory for other reasons.

Color - In renovation, consider changes in color. Different colors on each wall will make a room seem larger and may be useful aesthetically. Brilliant colors, such as flaming purple and bright reds, may be disturbing to many, but at least get away from the khaki and mauve colors that we used for too many years.

New Equipment - If you change space assignments in connection with renovation, you may need new equipment - charging desks, electronic detection systems, catalog cases, chairs and tables and more modern equipment, but do not forget the costs involved.

Avoid long tables because they are rarely filled. Few persons like to study at a table with more than four, and many, if they use such a table, prefer it with partitions dividing it into four. These can be just a few inches high to keep one's books from interfering with his neighbor's. If 10 inches high, they make it more difficult to see what your neighbor is doing and vice versa. If higher than 10 inches, they should be 22 to 24 inches above the table top, so that the reader will not be disturbed if a tall neighbor suddenly sits up straight and the top of his head comes into view. A sudden distraction is more disturbing than a continuous one.

Other new equipment may include audio-visual of various kinds and computerized automation which should be referred to an expert in that field.

If old chairs are worn out or uncomfortable and are to be replaced, consider these four points.

1. Comfort, as readers often sit in them for hours at a time.
2. Appearance, as few want to work under ugly conditions.
3. Price.
4. Sturdiness.

Too many libraries have chairs that look well but soon fall apart. Refrain from spending large sums on overstuffed furniture, which is very expensive and will inevitably induce slumber. A chair can be comfortable without being large or expensive. Too many of today's chairs with low backs are uncomfortable, particularly for tall persons.

A Flexible Building - Many older buildings are inflexible because of their many thick, load-bearing, interior walls which are expensive, if not impossible, to remove. If your renovation program makes the building as flexible as possible, your successor will be less unhappy about you.

Acoustics - Any renovation should deal with acoustics. Floor coverings which are worn out and impossible to replace with the original material such as cork and battleship linoleum have resulted in carpets in recent years. These are expensive. You can save money with them by using different color carpets where the wear and tear will be extremely heavy, such as on stairs, in front of service desks, and any place where people regularly turn in the same point at right angles and by replacing in these spots only. Would that we could buy the cork floors and battleship linoleum of two generations ago, some of which have lasted for 60 years and more, or the lifetime of 6 to 10 carpets, depending on the quality. But carpets do save in other ways. I am not opposing carpets any longer, but they are expensive.

Fire Hazards - Fire hazards continue, sometimes from carelessness and poor housekeeping, from cigarette butts in wastepaper baskets, or, in older buildings, from bookstacks designed with an air movement like that of a chimney. In new buildings we add to the danger with our proper desire for flexibility and fewer inner partitions.

Most buildings built before the Butler Library at Columbis, 45 years ago, had bookstacks with ventilation slits on both sides of each range. This dangerous chimney-like effect brought a demand for sprinklers and in turn oppositions by librarians who were more afraid of water than fire. Libraries are no longer built like chimneys.

Many libraries have smoke and heat detectors. Some have fire protection systems which flood the building with chemicals which smother the fire quickly, as well as staff and readers who do not leave promptly, but will not harm the books. However, recently other developments have expanded the fire problem into an economic problem. Halon, which is not toxic but which is very expensive to replace, smothers fire. Smoke and heat detectors sound an alarm and call attention to a fire before it has a chance to get out of control. Freezing wet books quickly before they have a chance to develop mold and then drying them out to just the right extent and at the right speed makes water from flood or sprinklers less of a hazard than in the past. As far as I know, we still lack an independent, unprejudiced study of the cost factors involved in these basically different methods, something which I hope will come soon. At present, I recommend Halon for very large collections of rare and difficult-to-replace books, but I would make the decision for the other material on the basis of estimated cost over a period of at least 15 to 25 years. The decision to install smoke and heat detectors or to install modern sprinklers that go off individually when the temperature drops to a safe level has important economic and operational implications.

This brings us back to to the original problem - to renovate a library or not. It is seldom an easy decision and should depend largely

on the cost of taking care of the eleven points that have just been discussed. It will differ for individual libraries. Find out what satisfactory renovation would cost and decide if it is worth putting that much
money into a satisfactory but probably temporary solution. In my experience, it is unusual for a library built before the First World War to be
worth enough as a library to warrant a large expenditure for renovation.
I can tell you of libraries built before the Second World War that have
been given up as libraries and used to advantage for other purposes, and
others where the same practice was followed except that the bookstacks
were kept for storage when required for less-used books. This plan may
postpone an addition to a new building for a good many years.

Extensive renovation should generally be carried out only when an
addition is also required, unless you think that microforms, compact
storage, and automation will make continued use of the present structure
possible. It may be unwise to add to an old building or to renovate it
if its site is no longer a suitable one, even if an addition is feasible.
The construction of the original building may make it difficult to add
to it without undue expense. The inflexible structure of the old building may make it impossible to provide suitable functional arrangements
and connections between the old building and an addition, which in turn
could make the addition more expensive.

Whether to renovate and add an addition to an old building or to
build a completely new one generally should depend on the cost involved.
New construction costs continue to mount. Funding is hard to obtain.
Satisfactory new sites are difficult to find, especially in our older u-
niversities. But remember, whatever you do - renovate, add or build anew -
keep the total long-run cost in mind. I realize that in many cases an
institution is not in a position to make decisions on cost alone but on
the availability of money at the time. Also, it is possible in most large
libraries to solve a space problem with decentralization without serious
effects, but that is another story.

Two final points - keep in mind aesthetic effects of your decisions.
They are worthwhile even if they cost money. The rewards for a satisfactory renovation will be great and should please you and everyone else
concerned. I have emphasized the difficulties simply because they are
too often forgotten.

University of British Columbia—
the decision to build an
underground addition

WILLIAM WATSON

Assistant Librarian,
Physical Planning and Development

Actually I'm here under somewhat false pretenses because I see I'm billed as describing an underground addition. It'll become clear that it was not quite an underground addition but rather a separate building that served the same function.

British Columbia is on Canada's Pacific coast. To the north are Alaska, the Yukon, and the Northwest Territories. The province of Alberta is on the east, and the states of Washington, Idaho, and Montana are to the south. It's a big territory, more than 366,000 square miles of mixed geographic and climatic zones, including rain forests, deserts, rangelands, and many ranges of mountains. British Columbia's primary resources are its forests, its minerals, its arable lands, and its seas. The population is sparse. There are fewer than two million people, half of whom are in Greater Vancouver. Two of every three British Columbians live in the southwest corner of the province. The rest are in small towns, most of them located in valleys.

The province is served by one large and two medium-sized universities, all located in the more populated southwest, and by a dozen colleges in widespread population centres. The principal university is the one named for the province and situated on the western tip of the Point Grey peninsula, part of Greater Vancouver. Like many universities, it developed from humble origins. It was chartered in 1908, but did not enroll its first students until 1915. It settled on Point Grey in 1925. Fifty years later it is a very different sort of thing. The campus is large and spread out. It offers programs in all of the humanities and social sciences, the pure and applied sciences, the professions, the creative arts, and who knows how many interdisciplinary studies. The student population this last year was 22,000, of whom 3,500 were accommodated on campus. The remaining five-sixths commute.

The University Library opened in 1925, establishing the centre of the campus. The Library stood out starkly against the raw land, but in

time landscaping softened the image; and, in the process, the angularity
became somewhat less awkward. The space in front of the building was
developed as lawn, and the centre of the campus was left clear and open
and, over time, became venerated.

The year 1925 you may know as the one when Clarence Darrow and William Jennings Bryan were adversaries in the Scopes trial. Vancouver, B.
C., is 2,600 miles from Dayton, Tennessee, but above the entrance to the
Library this contest is commemorated by two gargoyles. The one on your
left, his face sourly reflecting his theology, displays the banner of
Fundamentalism. The other, reminding us of our common origins, carries
the scroll of Evolution.

The interior of the Library in some of its aspects tended to out-
crypt Westminister Abbey. Elsewhere it was lavish in its use of space,
though for twenty years it was adequate to its purpose. The veterans returning at the end of World War II made it clear that the Library had to
be enlarged. The form of the addition, completed in 1948, was a north
wing, which more than doubled the building's capacity. In 1960 a south
wing was built, and a stack well was added on the rear of the Library.
All these changes presented problems of articulation. What had begun as
a rather ungainly and space-prodigal but straightforward building, became, by stages, confusing and difficult to use but grand and even state-
ly. By this time it was clear that the Library would not take any further additions.

Internally it had developed into divisions, some of them interrelated and others self-contained branches. One of the branches was the college library in the new south wing. Despite the fact that the collection
was awkwardly housed here and that the location was poor for providing
services, it was very heavily used. This was no surprise since the college library provided fewer than 500 seats for the Arts and Sciences undergraduates for whom it was intended and who numbered 7,000 when the Library opened.

From the early sixties on, the process began of solving the problem
of library growth by developing a system of external branches. Decentralization was adopted as a university policy for libraries. Between 1964
and 1969 seven new branches were opened. Now there are twelve external
branches and four others inside the Main Library. The Biomedical Library,
opened in 1964, has already been doubled by an addition. A new Law Library opened this January. Three other libraries are in different stages
of development.

Attempts to deal with the problem of library growth systematically,
by measuring, sampling, analyzing, forecasting, and documenting began at
U.B.C. ten years ago when we issued a plan for proposed library services.
We gave top priority to a library processing centre, second place to an
undergraduate library, and third place to a science library. To indicate
the impact of the proposals, only the second one has resulted in a building. The first is - ten years later - still in limbo, and the third has
simply been dismissed. Whether it is steadfastness or wrong-headedness I
don't care to say, but we continue to issue a series of planning documents. I am generally pessimistic about their impact. Though our ability to make accurate space predictions gets better and better, translating
them into the action that leads to solutions is more and more difficult.

In the increasingly horizontal university, procedures that are supposed to facilitate and enable, such as our manual on "Planning Co-ordinating Committees for Building Projects," too often frustrate and impede action. However, it is not every plan that comes to nothing.

In 1968 the Academic Planner forecast that in five years the U.B.C. student enrollment would have grown to 35,000. In response, the Library made an undergraduate library its top building priority, and the University authorized the preparation of a functional program. Traffic analyses showed that the ideal location for students would be just west of the Main Library. Architects viewed this area west of the Library and observed that distance obscured the fact that the Main Mall was twelve feet higher than the ground level in front of the Main Library. Why not build under the Mall? Moreover, they pointed out that the greenery could be preserved by terracing, and the trees could be preserved by putting them in containers. And that's what they did. The ground was excavated around each tree, leaving an area of thirty feet in diameter undisturbed. The exposed earth was encased in steel drums, and brick cylinders were built around the drums. The rest of the library was built to meet the drums.

There are only two bearing walls in the building: the north wall and the south wall. The rest of the building is post and beam construction. Precast columns were mounted on footings. Precast girders were placed across the columns, where they were locked into place. Double T beams were lowered by crane to span the girders on two levels. A slab was poured over the beams. A layer of waterproofing followed. The insulation was laid, and more waterproofing was added. Finally earth, lawn, shrubs, and concrete walkways finished the exterior. The edges of the building were mounted with concrete planters and filled with soil and shrubbery. On both the west and the east sides of the building courtyards were scooped out. Between the two courts the green of the lawn is carried through the building by the carpet. At the center of the building two inverted, truncated cones rise out of the Mall. The larger one, twelve feet high, contains the interior stairs. They were built by constructing a concrete cylinder with a large conical frame over it covered in carpet. Above the roof the cone becomes a skylight, which illuminates the lower floor. The smaller cone provides sunlight to the upper floor. Above ground the cones were covered with mirror glass. The trees help to organize the building. They define the traditional view down the Mall; and, two stories below, the large drums create similar streets.

On the upper level between the drums the streets lead to book returns, study areas, telephones, vending machines, and places to socialize. On the lower level the book collection fills the area between the drums, and the reading areas extend out to the east and west courts. Just inside the main entrance there are lockers and the entrance turnstiles. There is also a vending area and a coffee lounge. Further inside is the street to the north Mall staircase. There are coin-return lockers and some group-study cubicles. All of these elements are outside the library control point. There is a grill that can be let down after hours, so that the library proper can be closed while the outside area is still available for use. There are four exit and two entrance turnstiles. Right now they are being modified somewhat to accommodate a book security system. The long circulation counter leads in the direction of the reference counter. The reference collection is shelved immediately behind the counter. The counter itself faces in two directions. One part looks toward the circulation area, the entry and exit points, and the doorway to the lower floor. The other faces the catalog and the periodicals collection. On the way to the stairway to the lower floor is the recordings collection. There are 23,000 sound recordings housed there and 84 listening stations.

Because an environmental psychologist on the building committee urged that people need alternatives, two stairways were built side-by-side. One spirals down tightly. The other is more relaxed. Both stairways start at the same point, and end in the centre of the bookshelves. There is an aisle down the centre of the stacks that runs uninterrupted the length of the building. Lighting in the stacks is indirect. Fluorescent tubes were mounted on top of each stack section and a shield was added as the shelving installation was completed. This yields between thirty and forty footcandles at the lowest shelves. The bookshelves are flanked by consultation tables whose tops are at counter height. Beyond these are tables five feet in diameter. The area around them is open and largely uninterrupted. Also open is the area just east of the stairs. At the foot of the stairs, one looks out on the east court. At the windows there is a view of students on both sides of the glass. From a sitting position, one looks up toward the Main Library. There are quotations on the windows that are from Shakespeare and allude to glass. They provide a visual barrier to prevent students from walking into the windows.

One of the problems of the library was how to reduce to personal human scale an area designed to accommodate up to 1,400 students and only 200,000 volumes. One answer was to build platforms to raise the level of the floor in some areas. Walls of different heights were built, and many types of spaces were provided. To provide different environments, a variety of seating was provided. It was planned that some combination of walls and colors, floor height, and furniture arrangement would accommodate individual preferences. The intention was to make it possible for just about any student to find an environment to suit his temperament and mood. In two corners of the lower floor, the platforms were covered with carpet to invite the person who likes things casual. In another corner of the lower floor, group study cubicles are located in a glassed-off room. Each has a table for four and a chalkboard and pinning board. The staff work area is on the upper floor behind the service desks. There is a certain amount of privacy for the person seated at a desk.

How has the underground library been received? The students took to it immediately and almost without reserve, and it has been immensely popular with all its users. Indeed, aside from running-in problems and an engineering difficulty that had to be remedied, its only problems have been human ones. Specifically, some students are so sensitive that they will not ask others to be quiet, and others are so brash that they regard any such request as an infringement on their basic human rights. The staff are in the middle. Another matter that bothers me is that food and drink were permitted in the library proper, and now sandwich crumbs and drink rings are everywhere throughout the library system. Costs of operation are not perceived by the Physical Plant department to be appreciably different from conventional buildings. Altogether it has proved to be a good building. We regard it as a success.

SEDGEWICK LIBRARY, UNIVERSITY OF BRITISH COLUMBIA
VANCOUVER, B.C., CANADA

Sedgewick Librarian: Ture Erickson

Professional Staff: 7

Support Staff: 23

Student Assistants: 355 hours/week on a year-round average

The Library offers a standard range of services from 8:00 a.m. to 11:45 p.m. during the university terms (9:00 a.m. to 11:45 p.m. Saturday, and noon to 11:45 p.m. Sunday). It is open to general public.

Collections at the end of March 1975 numbered 140,000 catalogued and classified volumes, 23,000 sound recordings, and subscriptions to 545 periodicals.

Circulation transactions in the 1973-74 school year numbered 433,681. Recorded use of sound recordings, both on and off premises, was 247,147.

Sedgewick Library Building:

        Opened to the public: January 2, 1973
        Size: 113,349 gross sq.ft., 87,457 net assignable
                      sq.ft. net to gross ratio: 1:1.3
        Capacity: 200,000 volumes, 30,000 sound recordings
        Shelving: 1,541 standard sections
        Seating: There are 1,162 seats at carrels and tables,
                      84 at audio-carrels, and places for up to 500
                      on benches, hassocks, and built-ins.

Total project costs: $3,894,808

        Construction cost, including built-ins: $2,880,270
                    Furniture and equipment cost: $215,000
                                   Site cost: $199,496
                     Grounds development cost: $217,265
                                   Fees cost: $382,777

Total cost per gross square foot: $34.36

Total cost per net square foot: $44.53

Architects: Rhone and Iredale
Landscape Architects: Canadian Environmental Sciences
General Contractor: CANA Construction

The decision to build a new central library at the University of Texas at Austin

NANCY R. McADAMS

Library Facilities Planner,
University of Texas at Austin

INTRODUCTION

The preceding speakers have discussed the factors for and against renovation of an existing building, and additions to one. At The University of Texas at Austin we are in the midst of construction of a Social Sciences and Humanities Library to replace our Main Library in the University's famous tower. The process of deciding to build a new central library has taken years. During those years the library administration explored all the possible alternatives to a new building, and followed those which were right for the University.

By the end of the 1960s, with rapid growth of the University and the Library system, it had become obvious that the library could not continue to grow in the tower, and a new building was the only alternative remaining. Fortunately all the decision factors came together at a time when the University System administration was receptive to change and funding for construction was available. It was definitely a consensus decision at all levels - at the library administrative level, at the University administrative level, and at the System administrative level - and it was a decision which had strong popular support from students and faculty.

In retrospect one wonders why it took so long to face the inevitable. The probable reason is that the Main Library is located in the Main Building Tower, and the tower is the symbol of the University. The tower sits on a hilltop at the center of the original campus, the "forty acres." The campus has since expanded to the north and east to approximately three times its original size, so the tower is no longer the geographic center of the campus, but it remains the focal point of campus landscape vistas and it is a dominant element in the cityscape of Austin, a linear counterpoint to the rounded dome of the state Capitol, a mile away. It is hard to say what the tower represents to people - authority, education, culture, the joys of youth - but its mystique is powerful, so powerful that for a long time it obscured the fact that a very tall, very narrow building makes a very poor library.

THE MAIN BUILDING AND THE MAIN LIBRARY

The Main Building was constructed in the 1930s in two stages. The north element with the nine-story base of the tower was built in 1932, and a south element and the upper part of the tower were added in 1934. As a result the building is a complex maze of offset corridors and staircases, elevators that serve only certain floors or certain wings, light wells and courtyards, and it is further complicated by the need for cross-ventilation, a necessity in Texas before the days of air conditioning.

The entrances to the building are located at the first floor and one floor below, at ground level, but the entrance to the library is on the second floor, in a location which is not apparent from any building entrance. Thus the library is virtually unfindable by the uninitiated. The library reading rooms are located in part of the base of the building, along with various University administrative offices, and the stacks occupy much of the tower.

The structural system of the tower is a hybrid of multi-tier construction with concrete slab floors, using stack columns made of 4" x 4" structural steel angles on a grid 6'6" by 4'4". The 4'4" dimension defines range spacing, and the 6'6" dimension accommodates two stack sections, using a tubular steel intermediate support. The intermediate post is slotted to receive bracket shelving, and there are 1" x 1" slotted steel angles bolted to the 4" x 4" structural angles to hold the other ends of bracket shelves. An open space is retained around the perimeter of each floor for carrels.

Originally the library occupied levels 1 through 12. On these floors the walls and enclosures around pipe chases, ducts, stairs, elevators, etc., are of steel panels, painted battleship gray. There are unfinished concrete floors and ceilings, and the ceiling height is low - 7'4". The effect is very utilitarian, rather like being belowdecks on a ship. Above level 12 the floors are more conventional in appearance, with higher ceilings and plaster walls, but the same stack uprights continue upward on the 6'6" x 4'4" grid, all the way to the top of the tower.

Apparently it was intended that the entire tower be used someday for library stacks, but the vertical transportation systems go up only part of the way. Two passenger elevators which serve the office floors in the upper tower pass through the stacks but do not stop there, for reasons of library security. Within the stacks, readers and staff move vertically on the narrow interior stairs, which serve all levels 1 through 17, or on a tiny elevator which for some reason does not descend to level one, serving only levels 2 through 17. Booktrucks can be moved only on this small elevator. Books can be moved on a dumbwaiter-type booklift which serves all levels, or on the unique Snead distributor, an endless chain conveyor. Call slips for books to be paged for readers without stack admittance are sent to the stack floors by pneumatic tube, and the books returned via the Snead conveyor. The problem is that the pneumatic tube system and the Snead only reach levels 1 through 11.

DISADVANTAGES OF THE TOWER AS A LIBRARY

The disadvantages of the tower as a library facility are by now ob-

vious. The lack of vertical transportation is a severe problem, as is
the inadequacy of lighting within the stacks, and the shortage of reader
seating. The 400 carrels are doubly- and triply-assigned to graduate
students, and no faculty member is permitted a carrel assignment, so that
a faculty member may use materials within the stacks only by usurping a
vacant carrel.

There are serious service disadvantages as well. Since the stacks
are closed to undergraduates, and cannot be opened under the present circumstances, undergraduates must rely on the very large and difficult card
catalog, approximating 16 million cards, for access to the collection.
The arrangement of materials in the stacks is difficult because of the
small size of the floors. Levels 1 through 4, which extend into the base
of the building proper, hold about 80,000 volumes each, but levels 5
through 17 average only about 35,000 each. This floor size limits the
flexibility of the arrangement, complicates the shifting necessary to compensate for uneven growth, and makes logical juxtaposition of related materials almost impossible.

The worst problem of the tower, however, is one that no one likes to
think about - safety. The steel structure of the tower is not fireproofed.
All of the ductwork and most of the wiring is exposed. There are no heat
or smoke detectors, no sprinklers, no loudspeakers, and no alarm bells.
Until 1966, when a fire occurred in the tower, there were no fire hoses.
Firefighters had to drag hoses up the single exterior stair to the 22nd
floor. Now there are fire hose cabinets on every level, but they contain
dry standpipes, and must await the arrival of a fire truck before water is
available to extinguish a fire. Evacuation of readers and staff from the
tower would be extremely difficult, because of poor visibility, the hard-
to-find location of some stairs, and the fact that some stack levels fall
between Main Building floors, and lateral egress to another part of the
building is not possible.

ALTERNATIVES CONSIDERED AND FOLLOWED

By 1960 the pressures of growing enrollment had made it impossible to
provide efficient circulation service to students at the Main Library, especially to those denied entrance to the stacks. The University followed
the example of the University of Michigan and other large universities and
in 1963 opened an undergraduate library next door to the Main Building.
With an opening collection of 120,000 volumes and seats for 1,800 readers,
the undergraduate library removed crowds of readers from the Main Building
reading rooms, but it had practically no effect on circulation in the Main
Library, because enrollments continued to increase, and the proportion of
graduate to undergraduate students increased. Neither did the undergraduate library have any significant effect on stack space available for book
storage.

The next alternative, therefore, was remote storage. In the mid-1960s
the Collection Deposit Library was built, several blocks from the south
edge of the campus. With space for 900,000 volumes, it permitted the
transfer of little-used material from the Main Library and served the same
purpose for a number of branch libraries which were experiencing growing
pains.

The tower fire of 1966 provided additional incentive for the relocation of special collections and rare materials to modern fireproof buildings. In 1972 the Latin American Collection and the Texas History Center collections were moved to the new Sid Richardson Hall, part of a complex of buildings surrounding the Johnson presidential library; and the following year the Humanities Research Center opened, providing safe, secure storage space for all the University's rare materials. Space vacated by special and rare collections was converted to library processing space and to book storage, extending the stacks upward through level 17, to the upper limits of the elevator and booklift systems.

Through all this period a number of stack management techniques had been tried. Stack efficiency was very much assisted by our 1972 shift from Dewey to LC classification, which permitted compaction of the no-growth Dewey monographs; some of this low-use material is also fore-edged for greater stack utilization. Rearrangement of the entire contents of the stacks in the summer of 1974 was planned to provide just enough growth space to last until the move to the new building, without resorting to further compaction techniques.

ALTERNATIVES CONSIDERED AND REJECTED

Over the years there have been a number of proposals to expand the Main Building itself, and expand the library within it. All have proved to be too costly for the space gained. Other proposals have called for a new building for the University administration, with subsequent conversion of the entire Main Building to the library. These have been defeated by the Main Building's inherent traffic problems, the inaccessibility of some floors to the physically handicapped, and uncertainty about permissible floor loads, and by the symbolic view of the tower as the heart, and therefore the administrative seat, of the University.

Decentralization of collections has also been considered over the years, either by expansion of the branch library system or by replication of the central library collection in divisional libraries located in the growth sectors of the campus. The library administration has resisted this option because of its high costs for acquisitions and continued operations, and because of faculty endorsement over the years of the advantages of centralization to interdisciplinary scholarship. Texas' unusual funding base creates a situation in which construction funds are, at times, more certain than operating funds, and this factor has affected more than one library building decision.

The option of opening the stacks to all readers has been considered from time to time and rejected primarily for safety reasons, and because of limited seating.

THE FINAL ALTERNATIVE: A NEW BUILDING

At The University of Texas the need to face the decision about a new building came at a fortunate time. An opportunity to consider the problems of the library anew was presented by the appointment of two top admin-

istrators - a new Chancellor of the University System in 1970 and a new
President of the University in 1971. The library administration had of
course presented its view of the situation repeatedly in the past in annual and special reports. Their position was reinforced in 1968 by a
highly critical report made by a group of influential faculty members,
blaming the library's shortcomings on inadequate funding for acquisitions,
and inadequate space for processing and services, and reiterated by a 1970
survey of student and faculty attitudes toward the library. In response
to these reports a special committee was formed in 1970/71 to analyze the
library's space needs, define the requirements of a new central library
building, and to propose a site. This committee's report, strongly re-
commending a new building as the only means of achieving a first-rate library, was endorsed by the new President, forwarded to the System administration, and presented to the Board of Regents. In April of 1972 the Regents approved the project, allocated the funds, and appointed the architects.

IMPLEMENTATION OF THE PROJECT

After that the project moved very quickly. The library planning team
began at once to write a detailed program, based in part on the recommendations of the study committee and its several consultants, and to work
with the architects on the development of design concepts. By January
1973 the design was set, and by February 1974 the working drawings and
specifications were completed, approved by the Regents, and the project
put out for bids. In June 1974 the general contract was signed, with
1,000 calendar days allowed for completion of the building. As of this
time, the building is well ahead of schedule, with occupancy anticipated
in the late summer of 1977.

THE UNIVERSITY OF TEXAS AT AUSTIN
THE GENERAL LIBRARIES

Data sheet: SOCIAL SCIENCES AND HUMANITIES LIBRARY

Projected completion date: February, 1977
Projected occupancy date: July, 1977

Area, as calculated from contract documents:

Gross area, sq.ft.	500,673
Support area (includes air shafts, elevators, elevator lobbies, elevator penthouse, mechanical pump room, postal self service unit, primary switch gear, service entry, stairs, telephone and electrical closets, toilets, and transformer rooms)	85,505
Net assignable area, library functions	413,168

Efficiency= 82.6 percent

Volume capacity - 3,250,000 volumes

Reader seating - 2,800 seats

Project costs:

General construction, including landscaping	$17,427,371
Furniture and furnishings	2,700,000
Budget allocation: $1,500,000 for general furnishings, $750,000 for institutional procurement, $450,000 for carpet	
Future air balancing	51,000
Interface with other projects (utility tunnels)	126,255
Miscellaneous (building model, computer scheduling, printing)	42,700
Architects' fees	945,728
Administrative fees, UT System Office of Facilities Planning and Construction	406,946
Total	$21,700,000

Associated architects: Phelps, Simmons and Garza
                       and Associates, San Antonio, Texas

                       Bartlett Cocke and Associates, Inc.
                       San Antonio, Texas

Compiled for ALA/LAD/BES pre-conference, June 26-27, 1975,
by Nancy R. McAdams

THE UNIVERSITY OF TEXAS AT AUSTIN
THE GENERAL LIBRARIES

GROWTH IN TOTAL LIBRARY SPACE, 1964 - 1980+

	Gross Area Sq.Ft.	Reader Seats	Volume Capacity	Enroll-ment
1964 space:	362,505	4,484	2,187,470	22,196
New construction added 1964-1974:				
Branch libraries (Biology, Geology, Library Science, Physics, Communications, Engineering)	60,225	657	331,500	
Collections Deposit Library	62,045	89	925,000	
Special collections (Humanities Research Center, Latin American Collection, Texas History Center)	248,722	981	1,495,000	
Subtotal new construction	(370,992)	(1,727)	(2,751,500)	
Existing non-library space converted to library use 1964-1974:	5,710	222	12,000	
Existing library space released 1964-1974: (special collections and branches)	(-)42,619	(-)442	(-)221,370	
1975 space:	696,588	5,991	4,729,600	41,841
Construction in progress (late 1977 completion):				
Social Sciences and Humanities Library	490,000	2,818	3,250,000	
Chemistry and Pharmacy	11,900	155	77,350	
Existing library space to be released 1977-78: (Main Library and branches)	(-)141,290	(-)1,116	(-)1,165,500	
1978 space:	1,057,198	7,848	6,891,450	44,000 (est.)
Proposed for construction:				
Fine Arts Library	48,270	540	180,000	
Existing library space to be released 1978/80:	(-)4,545	(-)81	(-)19,000	
1980 space:	1,100,923	8,307	7,052,450	45,080 (est.)

Compiled for ALA/LAD/BES pre-conference, June 26-27,1975, by Nancy R. McAdams

DISCUSSION

Walsh: I'd like to make two comments, picking up on what Keyes Metcalf said. Bill Lamb, a lighting consultant with a national reputation who is based in Cambridge, has a phrase he often uses that I'd like to share with you. He said that the potential danger to your eyes of reading in low levels of illumination is as great as the potential danger to your ears in listening to soft music.

   The second thing concerns water-damaged materials after a fire, the bursting of a water pipe, or the like. We recently had a university library-wide committee develop a document on emergency procedures for the university library system. In a brain-storming session one of the members of the committee came up with a brilliant idea concerned with how we could interleave the water-damaged materials with clean newsprint and freeze them quickly, thus allowing time later to go through them and slowly handle them item by item. She suggested we call the student newspaper and the university food services. Both of them were more than eager to come to our rescue. The student newspaper said they had large quantities of clean newsprint in storage that they would be happy to rush over to any one of the libraries in case of water damage. The food services said that they would not only make room within the large freezers that house the meat for the student dining rooms, but, if necessary, they would call two or three of the large markets in the area, move their material to the suppliers, and let us use the freezers. That's something you might keep in mind in developing emergency procedures in your own system.

   I also have a question of Mr. Watson. Could you speak to the water table situation at the University of British Columbia and describe in more detail your waterproofing?

Watson: The water table does not present us with any kind of problem. It is apparently low enough so there is no danger of seepage. The original intention had been to put a lead shield on top of the building before some of the earth was placed on it. However, this had to be taken out for reasons of economy, and some kind of polyethylene was used. There have been several problems with seepage on a very small scale; none of them has damaged books yet.

   One of the problems of that building that occurs to me now that you have raised the question of the water table is that at one end sewage has to be pumped out, but at the other end it can drain naturally. When sewage has to be pumped, it always raises some kind of problem. Engineers have difficulty in resolving it.

Tjaden (directed to McAdams): You did't say anything about the use of the existing building. After you move out, are you going to retain the use of some of the stacks as a storage area?

McAdams: The answer is probably, we're not positive. There's really no
other appropriate use for the very large stack floors, one
through four, which run back into the base of the building,
about two-thirds of which are without windows. Their only use,
really, would be for the storage of small types of material, if
not used for books, perhaps for university archives. The university museum has asked if they might store zoological speci-
mens which can be kept in the dark and that seems appropriate.
As for the other floors, they will probably be converted into
offices. In those areas where the ceiling is a decent height,
that's at level nine where the ceiling shifts to 8'-4" as opposed to 7'-4". I'm in office space on level 21 now. It's comfortable enough. We do have transportation problems simply because there are more people that the elevators can handle. I
suspect that's what will happen. It's not for the library to say
what the disposition of the building will be.

Poole: I just wanted to make one comment about the freeze-drying of
books. If you can freeze-dry while the books are still wet, you
are better off not to interleave. The interleaving technique is
only useful when you cannot freeze-dry and when you use the interleaving technique to absorb the water which is present in the
wet books. If you are going to freeze, don't interleave. It is
helpful, especially when your books may have been embedded in
silt or debris or dirt, to wrap the individual volume before it
goes into freezing facilities, but don't do the interleaving if
you can freeze immediately. You'll find not only food lockers
in dining hall facilities and that sort of thing, but freezer
companies will also provide that kind of quick-freezing facility.

J. Park Randall: I enjoyed very much Mr. Metcalf. He's a rare individual.
The kind of consultant who is interested in the practical as well
as the aesthetic is rare indeed.

    Having remodeled a couple of old midwestern libraries, I
have a couple more things that we might add. A good place to
start, particularly if you are doing a feasibility study, is
with your new and more current building codes. It's amazing
what this can do to influence the decision to add to a building
and to determine what it will cost. It shouldn't be a last minute thing. You should start there. We found in the state of
Indiana, if you add to a building, any building, and spend more
money than 30% of the existing value of that building, you have
to bring the entire building up to current building codes.
That's ventilation; that's lighting; that's steps; that's hand-
rails; that's fire exits; it goes on and on and on. Sometimes it
can be a surprise that will defeat a building when it's ready to
be built.

    I also advise you to start with your insurance man; because
quite often, when you add to an existing building, even though
you're building of steel and concrete, the over-all rate will be
affected by the old building that you're patching. Be very cautious of that. We usually start there.

When I personally do a feasibility study, I start by having a visit to the building with a state fire marshal and a state building inspector. We go through, and we make a check list of all the things that we would have to do if we were going to build a building. I get the insurance man involved too. Sometimes you don't have to go any further. With those three people, it's a very inexpensive study.

Metcalf: I was very happy to hear the last speaker. There are other problems that we may have to face in the years immediately ahead. I heard this week that one of our states has passed a law saying that no library stack aisle could be less than 3 feet and 6 inches wide, so as to enable a crippled person in a wheelchair to use it. If this is done, it is going to add to the cost of our bookstacks approximately 15%. If this becomes a common practice, I think a group like this must take some action.

Orne: I speak at this point, because I was astonished somewhat by the shape of that building at Texas. You attributed it to the traffic control needs that the architect saw.

McAdams: No, traffic flow, external and internal, pedestrian and vehicular movement.

Orne: As I watch buildings, frequently when I see a building shaped like that one, I am sure the architect has gotten loose. It may not be so in this case. It may be that he's rationalizing from the traffic flow what he wants to do. That's not the point I was going to make though. I can only judge from the shape of the building and the planning I saw that you are committed to no expansion within that building or attached to that building.

McAdams: Not so, the whole west side is intended for expansion.

Orne: There is space there for it?

McAdams: The space becomes available when the adjacent building is removed, and the building is designed to be expanded in that direction, full library expansion through all six floors.

Orne: I was hopefully looking for a building without plans for expansion, another one, so we have examples to which to point.

McAdams: It will be a while. We expect it will take 15 years to fill it.

Vasi: I'd like to ask Mr. Watson the ceiling heights in the addition, especially in those areas where there are carpet-covered raised platforms. It appeared low but, perhaps, that was just a function of the great size.

Watson: It's actually not low. If you stood on top of the partitions, you couldn't reach the lower part of the ceiling anywhere with your hand.

Speaker from Cornell University: I'd like to go back to the flooding. One elementary point, if you ever have a flood as we did about five years ago, be sure the electric power is turned off before you go in after your books. We did not have a serious problem, but we did not think of it immediately. Fortunately no one was hurt.

Metcalf: I'd like to speak about the question of floor heights. I was amazed at the University of Texas with 7'4" ceiling. I thought they had basketball players at the University of Texas.

McAdams: I think they're readers.

Metcalf: I happen to be the tallest of my father's fourteen sons, and my son is six inches taller than I am; what's going to happen in the next generation I don't know. If you're building your buildings for the year 2000, you'd better watch your ceiling heights.

Realities—
funding of library
construction

INTRODUCTION

The only rational solution to many library space problems is new construction. Recognition of this fact is an important first step. The librarian is then faced with the powerful dilemma of limited availability of funds for social services and of energy shortages with its myriad implications toward conserving open space, conserving energy to construct a building, and conserving energy to operate it. This is further exacerbated today by another dilemma - inflation/recession.

The objective set for Dr. Beasley, professor of political science and former vice-president for economic affairs at the University of Texas, was to reveal to librarians the economic realities, as he saw them, for new buildings for libraries, and to indicate valid ways to successfully justify economic support of this alternative. His role was to help librarians gain further insight into the economic commitment of federal, state, and local governments, library trustees, and academic institutions toward library support. When is a library building problem viewed as a real problem by these bodies with funding power? How can librarians convince them that a problem exists and requires an economic investment to resolve it?

Unfortunately, the library space problem is usually interpreted as a book storage problem when it is in reality more complex and serious than this single deficiency. Other formidable building problems include:

1. Inadequate seating for population served
2. Inadequate space for staff, reducing efficiency, and resulting in increased operational costs
3. Structural and/or mechanical deficiencies posing potential life safety hazards
4. Poor environment posing problems of conservation for collections
5. High operational costs due to inadequate and inappropriate building structure
6. Poor service to public due to poor building configuration

What kind of data do librarians need, or what kind of approach must they develop, to substantiate the above problems which will at the same time convince funding bodies that a solution must be financed? Librarians need to develop a strategy to deal with the seemingly impossible dilemma confronting them and their potential construction projects.

Realities — funding
of library construction

KENNETH E. BEASLEY

Vice President for Academic Affairs
University of California

In my earlier days I conducted many workshops and training sessions
for public officials, such as this one; in fact I spent roughly half my
time doing that. We are in the process now at the University of Texas
at El Paso trying to solve our own library problems. I would like to
present three kinds of thoughts. One section is introductory, a second
section will deal with some external factors that are essentially beyond the control of libraries, the third will raise some questions devoted to discussions in progress regarding the saving of space as a solution. All of this is tied to funding, but I don't think that the locating of money is really the crucial issue we have at the present time.

Two introductory points must be noted in order to provide a background for later comments. The first was made by Harry Porrence, who is
the chairman of the Coordinating Board for all colleges and universities
in Texas, a very well-known editor, and, in many ways, an intellectual.
When he spoke at the first meeting of the Texas Association of Colleges
and Universities, he said

> I accept the premise that nothing. . . is as expensive
> as ignorance. But the plain fact is that the expense
> of acquiring knowledge and inspiration is about to
> catch up with it.

At the conclusion of his talk he said,

> I leave you with this admonition: If the financial
> burden of higher education becomes too heavy for the
> taxpayers, the long-feared advent of a new Dark Age
> will be closer than we think.

121

Although his views seem too negative and inappropriate for a library conference at the beginning of the third quarter of an amazing century, the speaker's concern is valid; and it is equally applicable to library service. Two decades of steady expansion, no matter how meritorious or long overdue, cannot be a realistic gauge to future development. Many people, including a number of professionals, are now saying that there is a definable saturation point in library service; and while expansion beyond this point might still have some net utility or social value, it declines rapidly and can easily become submarginal at any given time and place when compared to many other social needs.

Library buildings are a function of more complex interactions than are on-going programs, and the function can be expressed most easily by three short declarations, which most librarians would accept.

a. While library programs are more similar than dissimilar (regardless of community or institution), it does not follow that there are simple rules to determine the need or use of space.

b. Buildings are designed inevitably to support a current program, but it is also recognized that they constitute an important interim parameter for future programs; and they usually slow down the rate of change.

c. Decisions on buildings are made more slowly because the public resources allocated for them have more alternative social uses, ranging over as long a period as 10 to 20 years. Programs, in contrast, can generally be altered in a year with disruptions that are controllable. Programs are also mobile geographically while buildings are not.

Secondly, and almost contradictorily, there are for the most part adequate resources for libraries either nationally or in individual communities and institutions. When it is said that funds are not available for a library building or expanded program, what is really meant, increasingly so, is that the library program does not have a high enough social priority. This is true whether it's a public library or an academic library. In many ways we have been too successful in the library profession in the last decade and a half, because we have taught the public and the decision-makers what the standards are and the right questions that should be asked in developing the program, and now they're beginning to ask them. A low priority may be caused by essentially extraneous or non-meritorious reasons, such as the ineptness of a board, either public or board of regents, lack of adequate information by the public to support a reasonable decision, sometimes pathological social rigidity, and, on occasion, corruption. But on a national scale these causes are the exceptions.

The low priority is really relative. Advocates of all social services believe, just as most librarians do, that they are not being allowed to use their talents to the maximum to help society improve itself. For the most part, they are correct because, compared to the 1950s, society now has many more alternatives to choose from in allocating resources. Furthermore, most of the alternatives have equal value to each other in the short run or in the long run, whether the goal is to improve or change society in some way or to preserve social stability and maintain the status quo.

The competition that's forced by this condition will become more intense for libraries in the next two decades because of the nature of their service and because of certain demographic factors to be noted later. Library programs, more than other social services, are subject to incremental decision-making; they have more substitutes, and they are highly symbolic.

For example, the construction of a new public library building in El Paso or at the University of Texas at El Paso can be delayed for several years without any observable harm, although some special groups would be disadvantaged. The public library could make discrete decisions to add a special collection, dispose of a picture lending service, increase its newspaper collections, or reduce bookmobile service one day a week. These decisions would not affect the basic integrity of the total program.

The symbolism of library service is that it is considered essential in some form for a community; but, to satisfy the community, the form may vary tremendously. Libraries are also the handmaidens of the upper middle class, which usually sets an upper limit to the library program that's only slightly higher than the minimum. Indeed, no one knows for sure what the minimum or maximum is. Breaking this limit is difficult; and, when there is success, there is intense competition from segments of all classes who have strong and conflicting preferences about the development of all social services. The conflict is best seen in the public support for most library programs but a reluctance to demand new funding at the price of a reduction elsewhere. Library service is something one can believe in without making a commitment to act - like most religions.

While the generalization is true that there are sufficient funds for proper library development nationally and locally, there are exceptions. In any one locality at any one time, there may be insufficient resources for all social services, to the point that the locality is bankrupt. Illustrative of this situation are areas where there is (a) an exodus of people and physical resources resulting in the decay of communities, (b) an expansion of communities faster than services can be shifted, (c) confusion about long- and short-range goals, and (d) avoidance of uncertainties by decision-makers in an effort to maintain their political power, or more altruistically, to preserve political and social stability.

Here one gets into the broad area of community development (be it city, state, or institutional library) which cannot be examined at length in this paper. One can only note that the preservation of a mobile and free social system, with certain attendant and fundamental benefits, means dislocations in the sense noted above. In such dislocations, library service tends to suffer because of the short-run alternatives to it; and because, of all the social services, libraries are most akin to a fixed asset which cannot be moved at a social and physical cost less than its original value and can only be created within narrow limits. Their symbolic characteristic, therefore, nearly always causes a stronger fight to retain the library in one area than to create or enlarge a new one in another area where the social need is greater.

It is this dilemma which the library profession faces currently and will continue to face in the foreseeable future. It is this social reality which sets the first order of parameters for decision-making on the physical facilities of libraries. In this setting, with the increased educational level of the public, the old techniques of preaching need and using guilt feelings to spur action will only be marginally effective; and this new order makes mechanical standards, with which the profession has concerned itself in the past, of secondary importance.

Libraries have experienced their golden era for this century, and professional energy will have to focus on equal, and at times contradictory, measures of (a) economy, (b) development, and (c) aesthetics and comfort.

This seemingly obvious conclusion, to me, is not negativism and does not downgrade the role of libraries, but is merely a recognition of a new order which must be structured by professionals to preserve the civilizing characteristic of man with his innate aspiration to improve.

What must be considered in the rationale for assessing the problem of spatial needs? The major elements (a) are quite varied, (b) necessitate an assessment of social demands in as short a period as five years and as long as 20 years, and (c) encompass both theoretical views which define library service and the oft-times clashing applied decisions which set the design and pattern of actual use.

1. The first element we need to note raises the basic question whether more space will truly be needed in the future. Knowledge for the sake of knowledge is seriously being questioned at this time by society; education is once again becoming goal oriented; and the demand for the kind of research associated with libraries is declining. Contradictorily, there appears to be increased interest in our heritage and in forms of classical education (e.g., the general studies adult education degree).

How long this attitude will last is unknown, but two decades would not be an unreasonable expectation. This attitude is not anti-intellectualism, and it is not a denial of our inquiries into the nature of the universe and the creation of life. Rather it is a fear that we are destroying ourselves, that the form of our past inquiries will aid and abet that destruction, and that perhaps we as a people are still adolescents who need moments of rest in order to fill out parts of our identity.

For the library acceptance of these values for any extended period would almost certainly be a force for decentralization of materials and a much slower rate of growth. Largeness per se would not have the meaning of quality that it has today. Maintaining the currency of a wide variety of material would be less important, and immediate access would probably have a lower value. Already colleges and universities are reassessing their library needs in light of student shifts from one curriculum to another, and as it becomes more evident that there is a surplus of manpower in a number of the disciplines which, in the past, have needed certain specialized supportive library tools, they're beginning to change the demands and the needs at the institutions.

2. The impact of this apparent broad social change in attitudes and values is accentuated by some demographic changes that we'll see most notably in the 1980s and 1990s. They, too, raise the question about how much new space will truly be needed. Let me reiterate, we're not talking

here in a negative sense, and we are still talking about funding, but
we're talking about it in a broader sense of choices and of our alternatives.

Unless something very unusual occurs, there will be a steady state
era for libraries just as there will be for educational institutions in
the 1980s as a result of some major population changes. From now until
the year 2000 the age group under five is expected to be fairly constant,
if not declining. In the age group of 5 to 14 there will be a decrease
of about 5,000,000 children from 1970 to 1980, then a slight increase to
about the 1970 level by 1990 and extending through year 2000. Or to state
it differently, from now until the year 2000 the number of children between the ages of 5 to 14 is going to remain constant at the 1970 level.
Young people from age 15 to 24 are increasing in number during the 1970s,
but from 1980 to 1990 there will be a 6 million decrease, and by 2000 it
will have climbed to a little less than the 1970 level. The growth, from
1970 to 1990, will be an estimated 29 million jump in the age bracket of
25 to 45; this group will then drop slightly from 1990 to 2000. This is
a bulge that's moving through society. In the two age brackets of 45 to
65 and over 65 there will be a steady increase in absolute numbers (25
million) to year 2000, with the biggest gains being in retirees. Overall,
and equally important, is that the general population growth rate is now
only 7.5 per 1,000 population compared to a varying rate of 14.9 to 18.3
during the period of 1946 to 1962; and metropolitan growth from now until
the end of the century is expected to be from internal net growth and not
migration to the city. Another way to show the shifting is the fact that
high school enrollment will be fairly constant until the early 1980s, and
college enrollment is expected to be virtually the same in 1990 as in
1980.

Several obvious conclusions should come to your mind from even this
brief outline. The librarians, particularly the public librarians who
have objected to the sit-ins by students writing term papers and doing
homework assignments, will have a decade of restful relaxation. If this
age group follows the normal pattern of low library usage in early adult
years, there should be usage scars identifiable well into the 1990s. Increases in population over age 65 do not presage a drain on reading services. Changes in the lifestyle of libraries will then be primarily from
the growth in the 25- to 45-year-olds.

Based on current usage patterns, I estimate that per person usage in
the next several years will have to increase from 8 to 12 percent and maybe as high as 15 percent to maintain the current level of activity; and
the increase would have to occur despite the uncertainties noted earlier
about education and the obvious increase in competition for the time people allocate to reading.

Some buildings may become more commodious in another ten years, and
we may want to reassess the general standards we have been using. If the
nature of collections didn't change in this period - which partially determine spatial needs - I would be both surprised and sorry. A library
researcher at one of the library schools could and should provide a math-
ematical model for the profession to use in the next decade and a half for
planning at the regional level and, in some cases, at the city and county
levels.

3.   Alternatives to spatial needs are not set only by outside forces. Again, keep in mind that we have to determine what we need in terms related to funding; and basically, funding is available in the United States. We have resources. There are also internal forces over which the profession itself has control by direct decision-making or the education of the public. The most important one is a clear concept of and statement on what should be in the library, a more theoretical and yet more precise statement than what is available in the literature on selection policies. This is the part I mentioned a moment ago; we have been educating the public about what questions to ask as we have gone through this growth period of the 50s and 60s, and now they're beginning to ask them. What should be in the library? My personal conclusion is that current space shortages can be resolved fundamentally only if the profession addresses itself to this matter in a form understood by the public and decision-makers. There are three parts of the subject which can be examined today.

a.   First, there must be a recognition that, notwithstanding recent formulations of standards, growth is still equated with improvement and size with quality and ability to serve. No one denies the absolute growth in knowledge and the fact that a conflict-laden social system (based on advanced technology and urbanism) is less able to determine immediate needs and in turn generates more data. But this fact should not obscure another fact: that there is a determinable size at any one time for any one library arising from available time of people, educational level of the population, and the amount of social conflict in a community. This size can be measured by incremental additions in use compared to the incremental additions in the collection. Leaving aside the archival function, this determinable size is lower than generally conceded and places a high value on recent material and a theory of substitution of use. I do not like this conclusion, because I have the kind of curiosity characteristic of most librarians which demands access to all information fairly soon. But increasingly in recent years the insights into library measurement lead to a position that we are not distinguishing clearly enough (a) between functional need and quantity as a symbol of intellectual attainment, (b) between basic community use of materials and the inflated use coming from adding together a number of low-use and disparate services (records, pictures, story hours, meeting rooms), and (c) between activism to promote social change and the support of activities to help all people to decide what kind of society they want.

These comments are subject to misinterpretation as an advocacy of the status quo, but that is not the intent. All that is suggested is that the identity we developed (and I was an advocate of the new library order from the early 1950s to the early 1970s) probably cannot be the identity of the 1990s for the public, school, or academic libraries. Our trauma today is no different from the trauma many of us inflicted on the mossbacks of the early 1950s, except we are now intellectual mossbacks. A chicken in every pot and a car in every garage does not necessarily mean there should be a book in every room.

b.   Another theoretical way to view the need for material and
its relation to space is to examine a concept of use. A hypothesis
can be offered that the amount of material needed is a function of
(a) direct, frequent use and (b) infrequent but immediate demand use.
A library which implements both elements, as most libraries try to do
in some form, must inevitably continue to grow, given the present publishing culture; and systems will not be a significant deterrent,
given present standards for systems. Growth means new buildings in
the great majority of communities and institutions, since warehousing is feasible only for extremely large collections; and, anyway,
decentralization of large collections just shifts cost to current
operations.

Any modification of weighting of direct frequent use or infrequent immediate demand use will obviously alter the spatial requirements and character of many libraries. One thing to consider paren-
thetically in this regard is the change going on in education. Teaching at the elementary and secondary level now stresses the development of intellectual curiosity and its satisfaction through different
media and seeking specific material only when needed. Although reading improvement is a national program, it is my impression that teachers as a group are not as strong advocates of general reading in the
higher grades as they used to be. This educational attitude may be
objectionable to some people, but I do not think the students are
less prepared to be functional than other generations. It is more
realistic to accept the fact that reading for my generation was a necessity, and that speed-reading of memos which are soon to be forgotten plus other visual and aural stimuli will suffice for many a person for many years. Similarly, at the university level there is more
emphasis on progress toward a degree based on experience (i.e., successful cataloging of a conglomerate of experiences) translated into
successful test scores. As a specific illustration, not many political science teachers today expect a student to read the originals of
classics on political theory, and literature at the freshman level is
all that remains to encourage general reading for the great majority
of students.

It is quite possible, therefore, that print material will gradually change its symbolic form with much less concern about size as a
measure of intellectual security and a measure of self and community
advancement.

c.   In looking at size, therefore, one must interject some
thoughts about the publishing field. More and more in recent years,
I have been fascinated by the fact that the middleman in the knowledge industry is rarely discussed. He is a silent partner, and yet
he more often than not makes the initial decision on what knowledge
is disseminated and how it is distributed. His interaction with the
wholesalers and retailers (libraries) really determines the expansion
of knowledge. In economic terms, the publisher and librarian are in
a push-pull relationship in which library orders underwrite a distribution system much too costly to charge to an individual or even a
collection of consumers.

This underwriting or subsidization has merit because of its egal-

itarian character in that it enhances the competition of ideas even
though most ideas are read by very few people at a very high per
unit cost. In certain cases, the acquisition of material stemming
from this interaction reflects an economy of size and, therefore,
can often be justified. On the other hand, the publishers have an
incentive to proliferate publications and accordingly an internal
pressure to encourage libraries to acquire more items even though
there is a diseconomy of size and even though the value of each added unit is declining. University libraries are beginning to look at
this very seriously.

We compensate for this push-pull phenomenon in part by conceding
that scientific material becomes obsolete and should be stored (not
destroyed) and by a theory of weeding non-scientific material. My
impression of weeding is that the amount is set by quality standards
as modified strongly by the availability of existing space and the librarian's best judgment of the potential to increase it. In short, decision-makers are unaware that items are kept in different communities
according to factors unrelated to the theory of weeding. The evil of
underwriting, then, is not so much the acquisition of material, but
that it has obscured the need to retain specific items by diverting
personnel to acquire and handle the large volume of publications.

I am willing to argue that the life of fiction, biographies, and
pseudo-history books (ghost-written reminiscence) is much shorter than
conceded now; and that economy and the demands of an open social system can be balanced with smaller libraries. This advocacy in no way
reduces the importance of the library but rather enhances it because
the social consequences of poor selection and usage are more serious.
Phrased slightly differently as a question: Are space needs essentially set by an institution which because of its many components col-
lectively creates the need?

4. It would be wrong to deal only with theory involving braod cultural changes over a decade or two. There are some decisions under professional control (with a minimum of outside interference) pertaining to
the form of service and immediate use of space. For example:

a. An obvious decisional alternative is to give more weight to e-
conomy of scale by reducing the value placed on immediate access. The
outward manifestation of this approach would be (a) fewer but larger
structures in order to reduce unit costs, (b) an increase in the a-
mount of "mobile service," and (c) an acceptance of differentials in
service. Equality of service for libraries has been measured partly
by size but in practice more by the distance (in time or miles) one
lives from a designated size of collection. A simple change from a
travel time of 30 minutes to 60 minutes as a delineator of a service
area would have a profound impact on the nature and location of collections. In the 1960s I argued strongly for the 30-minute limit,
but I think that in the 1980s I will be accepting regretfully the 60-
minute limit and will be arguing that the expansion of educational activities by all social service will have diminished the need for the
elementary type of library service for which immediate access is important. In the past, we have assumed that this access is necessary
general library usage.

b.   Another related practical choice is to mold all libraries in an area into a rather rigid bureaucratic structure. This idea is not new and is probably no more palatable than when first proposed. It is nonetheless a viable approach which we need to discuss in the next few years. In El Paso, for example, it would mean eliminating the need for a major new branch facility (50,000 volumes), postpone the need for an expansion of the central public library building for 10 years, increase per unit use and correspondingly reduce per unit operating cost, permit the shifting of night-time studying to less expensive space, allow the concentration of specialists in quarters designed for them, and perhaps slow down the current rate of growth. Most important, the index of access and immediate usage would jump markedly.

On the negative side, institutional safeguards would have to be formulated to offset the loss of pluralism and the rather direct role consumers now play in setting the character of each library facility. Whether this loss would be fatal to a free library institution, I do not know. It seems to me, though, that the civilizing effect of public universal education, notwithstanding the perceptive views of Ivan Illich in his *Deschooling Society*, far exceeds the bureaucratic cost of schools molded into a centralized system. A convicted lawbreaker in one of the enlightened states is more likely to receive better rehabilitation with an integrated correction structure in which the judge can select the best unit to help him establish a new identity; and for all its faults, total mental health services have expanded the most in those states with well-established vertical structures, permitting easy movement of the patient from one milieu to another.

This reasoning and analogy leads directly to the question whether the decentralized library systems, which were the vehicle for moving library service from the nineteenth to the twentieth century, are now, some 51 years later, museum places, and a new vehicle needs to be designed. Fearfully, I believe that the answer is yes in many states.

c.   Related to some of the previous thoughts, but still independent, is a third possibility of the development of a new distributive system. I do not know what it would be, but it is clear that library service needs a location theory akin to the central-place theory in economic geography. For all of the research in recent years on library service, no one has examined the traditional assumptions about the behavior of patrons in terms of gaining access to an item of material. The assumptions are that (a) a person has multiple interests in materials, (b) he is stimulated by seeing material in which he had had no immediate interest, (c) access has to be relatively easy for him because his attention or demand span is low, and (d) use (interest) is a joint product of access to other primary social and economic services. These assumptions lead us in theory to one central integrated market.

But, if any of these assumptions are false, and I think they are, or if the behavior of patrons can be changed, new more economical distribution systems can be developed. For example, do libraries have

have to be located in/near shopping centers or other focal points of travel, all of these locations being high cost ones for buildings? Do libraries have to be in separate buildings? Can children's libraries be decentralized on a neighborhood basis in very-low-cost facilities open very selected hours? Should the library give up its recent programs in non-print materials to university extension centers or educational service units since one does not normally browse through this kind of material and normally does not use random search for items? Can some "discount houses" be set up whereby the material is cataloged and shelved properly, but no professional services are offered - one would learn by practice and simple directions which aisle had what he wants. Has the time arrived when evening public library hours in schools are a necessity? Would it be cheaper to duplicate material in school facilities rather than operate a fully independent public library system? The answers to these questions must come from patrons and citizens, with assistance from librarians, because they reflect value judgments on all social services.

   d.   Still closely related to the previous, but capable of independent implementation, is an examination of the role of fiction in libraries. From 25 to 40 per cent of a library's total volumes are in this category, and associated with this service is considerable space for traffic and browsing.

   Here again, not much can be done by libraries except on an *ad hoc* basis until a theoretical statement is formulated. It is not enough to say, as we do today, that fiction is important but that its value cannot be measured, even though both are true. We need an integrated statement which encompasses our knowledge of reading, general communication theory, therapeutic effect of reading, the recent trend to use the novel as a teaching tool in nearly all the behavioral sciences, and general learning theory. Also, there is evidence that the magnitude of current social problems requires the vehicle of the novel to both simplify and emotionalize complex subjects under controlled conditions of a vicarious experience. Also, no one has theorized yet about the present and future impact of higher educational levels on leisure reading.

   The substance of such a theory must address itself directly to such building issues as: (1) How much *traffic* space is needed to be functional or esthetic, or to satisfy a desire to parade affluence? (2) Do fiction collections need *prime* space? (3) Is it necessary to carry the *quantity* of material commonly held by libraries? (4) What are the standards of selection of material? (5) Is space for "advertising" new acquisition material justified (the new book shelf)? (6) Should the size of the fiction collections be inverse to the average income of the patrons and access to other sources - *i.e.*, should people be encouraged to use alternative sources for an item? (7) Can, as noted with children's collections, fiction material be located in low-cost neighborhood facilities with non-professionals as supervisors?

   My own reaction is that it is in this area that social needs to both economize and expand will force the biggest changes in library service.

e. Ms. Novak indicated in her letter that adequate staff space is also a problem. I agree, and I did not fully comprehend until preparing this paper that the library profession tends to incorporate into its building use, poor utilization of very-high-cost-space by locating professionals as often as possible in the main flow of traffic, so that they will be visible and available for consultation on professional matters. The employees are also expected to carry a set load of internal professional duties. Removal of the professional from immediate access to his/her material is heretical. But frankly, libraries are among the worst examples of designing buildings to try to do everything that is modern (from books to records to lounge to display to advertising to research to museum) and maintain the classical image of the library. These things can be done if the title is changed from "Library" to "Cultural Center" and sold to the public on that basis. It is not conservatism to say that some of the activities of the present library were started to meet an immediate need and to build up a varied clientele at a time when the middle class hungered for the simple life, *i.e.*, finding everything it wanted in one place.

As I have argued on other occasions, in the library of the future we must place more emphasis on self-help by the patrons, not only as an economy move, but to make the professionals' work more enjoyable and for the good of the patrons. In several libraries I have observed recently, as much as two to five percent of the space could be recaptured if office activities were placed at accessible points but in space designed for this purpose. Paraprofessionals, without desks, can be trained to do much of the public contact work and then refer the major questions of the patrons to the proper professional. The level of professional work would go up also.

Remember that hospitals, supermarkets, universities, museums, and national parks have found that patrons or clients are very hardy and can become fairly self-sufficient by training and repeated exposures.

Funding of library construction will be governed by future change, and the direction of that change will depend on the answers to the following questions:

1. What should the size of the collections be?
2. Will fewer people use the library, and should they be encouraged to use it?
3. How can cheaper structures to house libraries be provided; is decentralization, which would require smaller buildings, an appropriate solution?
4. Is immediate access necessary?
5. Can the concept of programs be reassessed for more effective response to current cultural and economic changes?
6. What kind and what form of material should be located in libraries?

If we decide that we do not want to change, then our task is, in some ways, relatively simple. We must go to the decision-makers, and we must explain and argue to them very strongly that the priority for the library must be much higher than it is now and must be much higher than many other social services. That will be very difficult to do, because they will be asking these questions that I've just indicated. As I said at the very outset, in terms of actual physical resources in the United States, we have the resources to do whatever we want to do. The difficulty is in setting the priority and convincing the people who are going to allocate it.

DISCUSSION

Beasley: We're going to have to re-examine our programs, in terms of the type of material we have. Let me make one other comment, because there is a tendency to assume that this is negative. I am pessimistic; there's no doubt about that. We're not going to change this in one year or two years. There's not going to be a big increase in funding, neither is there going to be a large decrease in the next few years. We're talking in terms of a decade, because that's roughly the order in which the population changes are occurring. When it comes to funding itself, I don't think there's going to be any doubt that libraries are going to have to be funded by all three levels of government. We might as well quit the argument or the discussions about trying to have a "local library." It cannot be funded that way given the attitudes of society at the present time on funding and our methods of getting taxes.

Roth: Dr. Beasley, I enjoyed your presentation. I'm a public librarian involved in research activity, and I'm concerned at the moment with some inconsistencies that I detect in your recommendations. The first point is the matter of change, the type of usage you referred to, the fact that you predict the need for 8 to 12%, perhaps 15%, of increased use to maintain current levels of activity. You then go on to list a whole group of other activities that may possibly become part and parcel of the library function. It leads me to believe, from the optimistic point of view, that this is going to give you more than your 8 to 12 to 15% increase in usage in certain areas. Also, the fact is that in our profession we are constantly undergoing change, and I'm afraid that you've generalized just enough at the moment to get everyone to sit down and say, "He's right. In my place I must do the same thing as somebody else is doing in Oshkosh." I think it would be important for you, therefore, to address yourself to the fact that each place has to be evaluated in terms of its priorities, its parameters, not generalize, which has been one of the major faults with the standards. That's the question. Could you please refer yourself to that aspect, the matter of usage? When you talked about fiction, I think it only fair to include fiction and general non-fiction, because the fiction area alone is still one of the smallest areas of purchase in libraries. In fact, it's larger in many academic institutions than it is in the public libraries at the present time. The non-fiction areas, or rather the general non-fiction areas, are growing rather extensively and that's the breadth of use as I see it at the moment.

Beasley: I don't really disagree basically with your comments. I've got to "cop out" on one part. In making a presentation like this where you're listening, and I've been on that side of the table many times, I do have to generalize. The written comments are more specific. Number two, I'm not necessarily advocating any of these things. Some of them I do not like; but I have to be, it seems to me, honest with myself, and I raise the questions with you. These are things that are occurring about which we have to make decisions. A number of them are contradictory, or mutually exclusive. This is the part I mentioned earlier when I said the profession is going to have to provide some leadership in answering these questions, or we will get a hodge-podge throughout the country in trying to arrive at some kind of an answer. That I would regret. If it occurs, I think we will lose, at least in terms of my experience (and I have worked with the legislature and public decision-makers in my current position) and in terms of funding required to keep up the field. These people are asking these kinds of questions, and they want an answer. They don't always see that they're contradictory.

Your comment about fiction I think is true, with one exception. In a large number of libraries, while it's not a high-cost item, it is a major space use; and it is designed this way. We're talking here about spatial needs. I just raise the question. Do we have to give prime space to the fiction collection as is done in many libraries? You can answer it either way. In El Paso, I probably would like to answer it yes, provided that they reduced it in Midland and Odessa so that we could have the money in El Paso. That's the kind of contradiction that you get among people. I do think it's a heavy, large space use and advertising space, but I may be wrong in this.

Diane Hjermstad: You seem to feel that systems are on their way out. As far as we're concerned, systems seem to be the answer to small libraries like ours. We're tied up with thirty-five libraries as well as Chicago Public Library. This gives us, through a union catalog, access to several hundred thousand volumes and, therefore, is an answer to space. Also, because we're connected by a band system and a telephone, we can have anything we want, usually within a couple of days. It seems to me that if we're going to talk about space and cost, systems really are the thing to come, with well-designed access between libraries. Would you tell us why you feel systems are on their way out when the developing systems, such as the North Suburban Library System that we're in, are really the answer to our space problems?

Beasley: No, I don't argue that systems are out. I am also smart enough
           not to ever advocate that. I do think, as I was trying to sug-
           gest, that there is a preoccupation in the library profession
           with the concept of systems. They were a very useful tool, but
           I think we have gotten to the point where we have assumed that is
           the end-product. I'm suggesting that we need now to build on the
           systems, and it may change the character of our concept of sys-
           tems. But by the 1990s the systems are not going to look like
           they do now. This in no way is against the systems. The sys-
           tems will not change basically the spatial needs of the library.
           That's obvious because we're meeting here today, and I suspect
           that if we went around the room here, those states that have good
           systems have as much of a problem with space needs as those
           states that do not have systems. Systems won't solve that prob-
           lem, but that doesn't mean that systems won't solve other prob-
           lems. I think we're coming very close to making systems the end
           object in the library profession.

Roth: What about the regionalization development that's taking place?
         What about regionalization concepts with different types of li-
         braries working together: academic, public, school, etc.?

Beasley: This is the part where I think the public decision-makers are
           going to force us to do something if we don't do it as a profes-
           sion. In that way you can make a significant impact, for exam-
           ple, on space needs, the subject we're discussing today. As I
           was indicating in my comment using El Paso as an example, if you
           create a strong regional cooperative system involving all forms
           of libraries, it would have a tremendous impact in this communi-
           ty of approximately 450,000 right now. Remember, I indicated
           that we could eliminate the need for a branch; we could elimi-
           nate expanding the central library for at least ten years.
           Those kinds of things really make an impact on a decision-maker.
           Here is what I think we're going to be forced to do, and we will
           have no choice.

Rift: I totally agree with you that libraries have to justify the higher
         priority in the social scheme in order to have more funds avail-
         able. But I do not share with you the pessimism. I know that
         several public libraries are becoming both the social and cul-
         tural centers within their communities. As far as my own spe-
         cial situation goes, I know of others, like my college library,
         where the college has really become the center, more so lately.
         We have become a much more integrated part of the instructional
         process. In fact, this is where our main problem lies when it
         comes to space, because we have so many more activities happen-
         ing in the library today and internally the percentage of total
         funds has remained steady. The needs have increased to such an
         extent that we are constantly looking for external funds which
         are not available.

Beasley: When you get down to specific situations, this may well be true.
          When you talk about what is going on in the U.S.S.R., whether one
          is optimistic or pessimistic is based on how one puts the facts
          together. There's one part that I don't think we can deny or es-
          cape. In the 1980s we will discover that we have grossly over-
          built educational facilities in the United States, and there's
          going to be many a university library or college library that's
          going to be up for sale, distribution, etc., because we're going
          to have to close down institutions. We're already talking about
          it. In several states they're making plans to close down entire
          institutions. This is bound to have some impact on the rest of
          the development of the profession. I can give you one state now
          where there are at least three or four institutions that will ei-
          ther have to close down or there will have to be tremendous infu-
          sions of federal money in order to keep them going. The cost of
          maintaining those institutions per student, or per credit hour,
          would be so out of line that I don't think the public would buy
          it. I would suspect that in a few areas this is true in the pub-
          lic library field, that we have overbuilt.

Orne: I'd like to say first that I enjoyed everything you said because
       you agree with everything I think.

Beasley: Let's get together more often.

Orne: I don't read what you say as pessimism at all; I think it's realism.
       Very early in your talk you alluded to the fact that many of the
       things that you were going to say you didn't like. I would sug-
       gest that when you were only a professor and not an administra-
       tive officer your reactions or actions were quite different from
       what they are now. I've seen both of these in quantity over the
       years as an academic librarian, and I appreciate very much what
       your attitude has become and understand the basis for it. It
       seems to me unfortunate in a place like this, in a group like
       this, that we have to have a professor and an academic officer
       come to tell us the facts of life, that librarians themselves
       should have thought of and expressed as well as you have. Thank
       you very much.

Beasley: I can't take all of that praise, because you have to remember
          that it was the professors and the academic administrators who
          did not see the plateauing of enrollment in the 70s and, not un-
          til the enrollment plateaued did we understand what was going on
          in the 1980s. And then we suddenly started looking at the fig-
          ures. I think it's one of those things that crept up on us, but
          it is amazing what is likely to occur.

Metcalf: We've had a very interesting and very worthwhile talk that
          ought to be good for all of us. I would like to say, however,
          that libraries have made a good many improvements in the last
          forty years. We have shifted in our university libraries from

75% to 50% professionals on our staff, many of us to 25%, which has saved a tremendous amount of money. We have developed cooperation. We've reduced the cost of cataloging; or at least reduced it in relation to other costs. We have been forced by university administrative officials to spread out into new fields, worthlessly. We have been forced to build extravagant buildings that have cost hundreds of millions of dollars. I've worked on a billion and a half dollars worth of buildings that could have been built for a billion dollars just as well as not. One thing after another of this kind has happened. It's going to be very good for us to be hard up for a short time. We're going to be hard up for a longer time, because of the change in population growth. We need to take the advice that we've been given, and our university officials and our head librarians have got to get together and understand each other more. One of our great problems throughout the country has been that the administrative officials had always been afraid of libraries because of their cost and have refused to talk things over with them sufficiently so that they understood each other. I've worked for five hundred libraries and have a feeling for the subject, but I think we're coming along and I'm not a pessimist at all. We're going to have a hard time the rest of this century. I wish we could get over it in five years, but because of the population it is going to take longer.

A view from outside—
running out of space,
an alternative

INTRODUCTION

Robert Propst devotes his energies to research programs to solve
problems in facilities management. One of the products of his research
is a publication "High School: the process and the place," a report
from Educational Facilities Laboratories; another is "The Office - a
facility based on change." Planning principles developed in these publications can be applied to existing library buildings to achieve
increased utilization of space and to develop an efficient, economical
method of changing that space.

However, Propst did not emphasize the space-saving aspects of his
planning principles in his presentation. Instead he placed his emphasis
on change and human needs, leaving for his colleague, Doug Englebart,
the task of telling the audience how change will affect the library's
collections and how space-savings can, must, and will be realized.

The theme, a view from outside, was intended to provide another dimension in the understanding of library space problems. Views from individuals committed to problem-solving, such as Propst and Englebart, provide an opportunity for librarians to see their institution in a new
light. This is especially true because we are all, in our own ways, in
pursuit of solutions to effectively store and communicate information in
a radically changing environment. The solutions that Propst and Englebart are developing will help libraries to cope with their problem.

137

Human needs
and working places

ROBERT PROPST

Herman Miller Research Corporation

In our knowledge-based society, institutional workplaces such as offices, schools, and hospitals are great social inventions. They are the vast continuous showplaces where society interacts.

When we go to work or when we go to school we go with some expectation that we will be a part of something of consequence. The degree to which we are able to participate, to contribute, to be known and valued, is a major measure of human satisfaction.

But how well do we know the school or the workplace? They have suffered from being too close and too familiar - literally under our noses, within sight and touch. Little attention has been paid to the physical environment because of overfamiliarity with its overt characteristics but also because of the tendency of physical arrangements to static formality. There is also a widespread assumption that physical settings have little impact on organizational functioning.

We are beginning to discover that, on the contrary, the immediate physical environment has great influence on organizational life. It may often be an active cause of organizational decay and failure. It is emerging as an influence which we must learn to manage and use in productive ways:

> I spent my life as a psychologist, trying to figure out
> ways in which I could change people or enable them to
> change. I did it, first of all, through individual psy-
> chotherapy, which was my interest for a number of years.

This paper was originally presented at a symposium on Management and the Working Environment in London, September 21, 1972. The symposium was sponsored by the National Association of Mental Health. It has also been published in a monograph entitled "Learning Environments."

Then I began to see that that's not as potent as group work perhaps would be, so I got interested in groups. Then I found that you can't really change people that way - you have to understand whole organizations. So I became interested in organizations. Finally, I got interested in environments, because no matter what scale you work on, you can't reform people, you can only create new forms. But people do change. They change almost entirely, according to the situations in which they find themselves. It's not trimming people need - it's liberating. And environments can be very liberating.... Let's go into the institutions and organizations and see if we can't arrange the kind of social architecture that would...enable people to become what they want to be in everyday situations.[1]

How do we live and work? What matters? Here we face a vacuum in language and values. But we can start with a definite goal - to improve the *satisfaction* and *proficiency* of those who work. To determine if we are achieving this objective we can apply a simple test to the work or school environment: Would I go to this place even if I did not have to?

There are several key issues for educators and designers, a new team who must now begin to work together with a great deal more understanding. The perception of these issues by decision-makers may have significant effects on life in organizations. The first is perhaps the most unexpected and disturbing.

Possession: "Can This Place Be Mine?"

Members of a better-educated, more participatory society no longer view the places where they work as the sole possession of others - the bosses or owners. There is an increasing consensus that a place and an activity which consume a major portion of an individual's life should in a very real sense be "possessable." This immediately raises questions: Can we let office workers and administrators possess offices? Are we not afraid that people, unpredictable, tasteless, immoderate, chaotic, will be corrupters of public places?

But new thinkers are asking other questions: Are not public places as we have conceived them, cold, defensive, untouchable, geared to the worst possible behavior, corrupters of people? We are learning that with a new philosophy of facility expression we can indeed allow students and workers possession of their workplaces if we act with candor, confidence, and understanding. In many ways the key to a meaningful involvement with work/learning is to know that the workplace "can be mine."

Once managers and designers accept this philosophy the physical workplace can take on remarkable new qualities which we can all endorse. It can become a bright, fresh, human-scaled, comfortable, responsive environment which advertises its willingness to be possessed by "me."

[1] Richard Farson, "The Greatest Realization," *Environmental Planning and Design*, vol. 8, no. 3 (September 1970).

Manipulation: "Can I Adjust Anything to My Needs?"

Managers and educators must next ask themselves: Can we allow a public place to be changed or adjusted by its users? Will any kind of logic, consensus, or acceptable formality prevail? Or is this the road to confusion and chaos? New experience is showing that each of us possesses an order-seeking sense although in most of us it is a dormant, untrained capability. (We have been conditioned to the reverse - do not touch! do not use!) A lively manipulation of the work environment can support the uniqueness and variety of both the individual worker and the tasks he performs.

This new user-influenced environment will not result in less discipline or less agreement with the orderly processes of the organization. It is, in fact, a new level of agreement permitting the individual to implement a broader spectrum of changes at his discretion. In a curious way, it is agreement that managers may also manipulate the work environment to meet the dynamic needs of contemporary organizations.

Work Process: "Can I Produce Results?"

The most stilted and harmful concept of work function is the view that it is supported by a static facility to be put in place and then populated by equally static and hypothetical people with attendant sedentary activities. Facility designers have tended to be oblivious to or unattracted by the analysis of the work and learning process and have delivered schools and workplaces that are neither effective nor comfortable for real people and their dynamic affairs.

The result is a serious process inhibition. For example, the usual focus on rushing information into classified storage has given office work a false sense of process effectiveness. But information in storage is *information out of process*. The result is a well-documented expensive death and burial of information in files and computers. This is very much akin to a factory concentrating on raw-material warehousing while ignoring the production and delivery of a product.

Process! Process! What does this mean to school and office facility function? A good process has a high proportion of its product being acted on at any given time. In schools and offices this product is information. If information is being acted upon, it is likely to be out of its storage mode. If it is out of a storage mode, it is likely to be visible, audible, and tangible in the work environment, and it is likely to be in some transmission mode most of the time.

So we arrive at a new type of function for the work environment, the business of supporting information transaction. This means more display, more accommodation of work generation, more transportation and manipulation of communication facsimiles. It is more attuned to "work station" concepts which provide the hundreds of specialized work functions that must be designed and generated on the spot. The concept of office function as alive and, to a large degree, characterized by a kind of organic organized process is a new facility need we should understand and endorse.

The Social Structure: "How Can I Relate to Others?"

Any good manager understands the enormous potential in the chemistry of human relationships. Organizations are structured along lines
that propose to make combinations of people effective. Now there is a
growing awareness of the equally compelling influence our direct physical surroundings have on this chemistry. We are, more than we have
suspected, the product of our surroundings. We act and communicate as
our environment directs. The fact that school or work environments have
become design stereotypes does not mean that they do not still compel
behavior and influence social interaction or communication events. Pre-
dictably, there are accidents, occasionally good, but more often bad in
their effects.

In simplest terms, the physical items that fill an office, school,
or any public building help make social and communication statements.
Zones are established, boundaries are determined, access and exposure
to associates and to information are provided. To a shallow-thinking
planner, design is simply a matter of obvious geometry with a status
hierarchy overlay. To the facility user, it is a far more crucial matter.

It is now well established that work spaces and equipment can be
structured to fit the true communication needs of an organization. This
is a game, fluid and complex in nature. As communication groups are recognized and located, definable territories marked by definite perime-
ters or enclosures can be developed to support them. But these developments almost immediately come into conflict with an overmethodical or
rectilinear organization of space. Thus we are seeing the rise of a new
kind of geometry - many sided, with openings and access fortuituously located, and utilizing a whole new vocabulary of space-modulating hardware.

Traffic itself is also recognized now as part of the communications
and social effect in an organization: getting around, who we see, and
how often is a powerful communication leverage that can no longer be left
to chance. This introduces another component to the manipulation of
space - the design of movement that is not only efficient but also generates vigorous communication interaction as part of traffic activity.

Change Effect - Cost and Consequence: "Can I Afford It?"

The bane of most facility managers is change of any kind in the physical facility. Unless a volcano of pressures for change develops, it
rarely seems worth the trouble, confusion, dust, and downtime. This
"trouble/cost" consequence is so ingrained that interior reordering often
lags seriously behind the point where organizations actually need change.
In other words, the "penalty" syndrome is so pervasive that people and
services will stay put for months and years in arrangements that have out-
lived their usefulness.

With new interior systems that *forgive* easily, this inhibition disap-
pears. For the first time, changes in facility and interior design can
match the desired change rate of organizations. With this sudden step forward after many years of negative conditioning, we are still underestimat-
ing the potential for fast response which results from firsthand adjust-

ment by the user himself. Assuming that any large organization is undergoing an almost continuous restructuring of group size and relationships, the phenomenon of continuous interior shift is both realistic and
possible - if the interior system is designed to meet this kind of on-
going negotiation.

Beyond simply relieving the pressure on users to accommodate their
activities to obsolete arrangements, there are other, less obvious advantages of a change-oriented approach to interior design. If we dis-
card the planning myth of "perfect" numbers of people supposedly occupy-
ing "perfectly" methodical space, the user can now occupy space elasti-
cally with numbers varying to suit the moment. By storing extra space
in corridors and service areas, actual space used by humans individually
or in groups can have a new kind of perfection. It can indeed have the
right size, shape, and orientation for each communication interaction.

A second factor of equal importance in change accommodation is the
refreshing effect relocation has on individuals and the organization itself. The hazard of long-term static location of office users in set-
piece facilities is the rather rapid exhaustion of novelty in the interaction of people. When group A moves next to group B, their interactions
will be fueled by the fact that individuals are trading fresh information
and viewpoints with each other, but only for about six months, at the
most. Vitality, mobility, and new ideas are the important by-products of
this fresh association. But after a period any individual or group begins to exhaust the novelty of the ideas of another individual or group.
Relationships may continue on a smooth operating basis for years on end,
but it may well be only cog turning. This factor alone is cause enough
for fairly frequent moves and restructurings of physical facilities. It
far outweighs in value the temporary insecurity and drop in proficiency
which change might bring.

The Aesthetic: "Is It Beautiful?"

The appearance of offices and schools has been frustrating to both
designers and users because of a conflict in cultural values. We have
refused to accept people and work as part of the natural appearance of a
workplace. Rather we have labored under the delusion that the only time
an office or school looks "good" is when all signs of work underway and
the people engaged in that work have somehow been concealed from view.

At the heart of a new view of workplaces lies the contrary premise
that things natural, interesting, and relevant to man at work can also be
beautiful. We must begin to see that people and their ongoing work are
the bases from which the natural beauty of a facility must spring. The
designer must embrace furniture, facilities, and services in this context
and cause it to be a key to an emerging aesthetic for office and school.

The workplaces of unique and strong-minded individuals show us the
way. They have never allowed their surroundings to become the mannered
statements of strangers. They have possessed their workplaces, and their
character, purpose, and goals are clearly reflected in their direct environment.

It may be difficult to step through the looking glass from an unreal

world of manneristic and disconnected impressions of the workplace to
a real world of user possession, manipulation, process, social and communication structures, change accommodation, and the natural look of
people and their work. But this is a more plausible, comfortable, and
functional world. It involves making the physical environment into a
more expressive and sensitive tool, a tool to be shaped by the user
himself. The user, expressed in terms of both the individual and the
larger organization, will receive new satisfactions and proficiencies
as a result.

Running out of space, an alternative

DOUG ENGLEBART

Director, Augmentation Research Center

Long-Term Strategy for Augmenting Knowledge Workers

I've been on a fairly single-minded pursuit for 24 years. It is centered about trying to improve the effectiveness of institutions for coping with the complexity and urgency of the problems they face. When one thinks of this complexity and urgency, it soon boils down to problems of the knowledge workers as associated with sorting out the information, making a plan, making commitments, marshaling the resources, organizing the people, managing, monitoring, watching.

To improve what knowledge workers can do, we've developed some fairly radical computer aids, in transitional stages, first for individuals, then for small teams, and now for communities of up to 50 people, distributed about the country. Through these stages we find many common knowledge-based activities, and we assume that the system we use serves as a reasonable prototype for gauging some of the possibilities ahead for the libraries and their related institutions. The same knowledge workers whose augmentation we are exploring will be providing the input to the future libraries, and they will also be the libraries' customers. Assumedly, the goal is to improve the effectiveness of these knowledge workers. It is quite clear from my experiences that they as individuals, teams, and special-interest communities will be augmented heavily with computer aids, and that this will affect the evolution of the libraries.

My long-term pursuit of a coherent goal, involving relatively large changes in the working lives and institutions of people, has brought to me a number of perceptions about institutional evolution that may be worth sharing with you. So, before dealing with some specific technological possibilities, let me introduce some other thoughts bearing potentially upon your future.

145

Size and Similitude

Hidden down in the stacks of the library some place, there are books
and articles about a topic called "similitude." It is something that the
engineers and physicists developed a number of years ago to cope with the
fact that devices and equipment don't behave the same when their physical
size is changed significantly. You are all aware perhaps that an exact
scale model of an airplane may not fly at all, even if the original is
perfectly airworthy. Similitude is the art of determining what conditions can be imposed upon dimensional scaling in order to obtain similar
behavior in different-sized models.

It turns out that as the physical size of something is changed, for
instance if every linear dimension is multiplied by the factor x, then
the area of any part would change by a factor of x-cubed. Phenomena upon
which the workings of the thing depend will depend in turn upon volume in
one way and area in another; while the co-working of these different phenomena produces the workings of the whole. Change the scale and the different phenomena upon which the working depends will shift their behavior
in different ways until a point is reached where they no longer cooperate
as necessary to support the original way the things work.

Consider a sampling of such effects: the impact upon you and your
immediate environment if this meeting room and everything in it, including
yourselves, were suddenly to be made larger in every linear dimension by a
factor of ten. What would you notice, and how long before you noticed it?

This meeting hall has some heavy chandeliers hanging over your heads.
Since their volumes are a thousand times as great, their weight has increased a thousandfold. Their support chains have a suspension strength
proportional to their cross-sectional areas - they will be a hundred times
as strong, but must bear a thousand times the weight. It is unlikely that
their present design carries a ten-to-one safety factor. Their crash
would be noticeable, no doubt. But you would likely be preoccupied by the
collapse of your chairs, which also aren't designed with a ten-to-one safety factor. Would you scramble to your feet in alarm? Hardly. Your bones
and muscles aren't designed for a tenfold increase in apparent body weight,
either. Would you shout for help? Well, you would be very short of
breath on the one hand, since the surface area of your lungs probably can't
serve proportionally ten times the oxygen demand; and on the other hand,
your speech mechanisms are hardly likely to be manageable.

Galileo apparently calculated a maximum height that a tree could at-
tain, based upon the limiting strength of the wood as the geometrical factors scaled up. This was before the giant redwood trees were discovered;
and they just about reach his limit. Biologists have noted that small
mammals can't survive in the arctic regions where the proportion of heat-
draining body area to heat-producing body volume becomes too large for
them.

I first became interested in similitude because of scaling problems
with an electronic device that I was working on - it became inoperative
when the size was reduced below a certain level, otherwise it would
have been a beautiful candidate for a very highly miniaturized computer
component. So we see that the same sort of problems are met when sizes

are changed in mechanical objects, electronic components, and biological organisms. Without making too much of a case for it, I submit that man's institutions must also be subject to similar natural laws. The steady increase in scale of total quantity, rate of production, and access requests for our recorded knowledge is bound to hit limits where the current form of our libraries simply cannot function.

The Library as a Document Warehouse Is Doomed

I'm not sure that anyone believes that libraries can continue storing in full-document form all of the recorded documents that are relevant by today's standards of librarianship. Double the number of scholars and there will be twice the service demand on double the amount of information flow - service problem scaling by x-squared. In n years, the accumulated collection will double, but I'll bet that cost for accessing a book or journal paper will not be double (as if a second library matching today's could handle the new half), but will be more like four to eight times as great. Earlier today, I heard Dr. Beasley say that librarians and the public are going to have to accept a change from 30-minute access to 60 minutes. How many years until the access time again has to double?

I have been invited today to bring to you an outsider's view of the library world. Well, I think that the library as a document warehouse is doomed. There is no way, in my view, that the present institutional mode of service can continue to function as the scale of knowledge and knowledge-based activity continues indefinitely to expand. But many things in our life today are similarly doomed; the thing to do is to accept that some basic changes must occur, and to try to bet on the right approach.

I perceive two types of librarians:

1. Librarians who like libraries and whose entire image is submerged in working and supporting that traditional institution.
2. Librarians who perceive their role as supporting the recorded dialogue taking place in society, who understand that the dynamics required for that role are going to change and the structure of the institutions to support it are going to change, and who are committed to serve in that role regardless of the changes in institutional structure.

As I see it, the first type will have a great deal of difficulty during the transition period and will eventually disappear; the second will not only adapt readily but will flourish in the library future.

Environment and Environmental Changes

I will tell you next about some of the environmental things that lead me to think that if scale doesn't destroy the library as we know it, there are other things in the environment that will. Maybe today's librarians will have all retired by the time it happens. However, if they have allegiance to the long-term institutional need by society for support of its recorded dialog, they'd be copping-out if they didn't begin now to orient

themselves for the transitions ahead, to accept the inevitability of
change in form forced by change in scale, and to begin integrating that
inevitability into the way they approach today's problems.

Historical-Technological Change

Before we leave the question of scale and the fact that the sheer
mass of stored documents will eventually founder today's library system -
consider what happened to librarians when clay tablets began to present
a storage problem. A new technology - using paper-like devices - seemed
to be emerging but wasn't very acceptable for various reasons. If you
talked to the poor old bent-backed guy who had to handle all those clay
tablets all the time, and worry about their maintenance, you would wonder
why he was so hooked on them. "Well, look," he says, "that's the way all
those guys write. They hand me the stuff. What else am I supposed to do?"

Conserve Resources, Cry "Pollution"

Are you really the helpless victim of the tablet producers - or today,
of the document producers? Must you really keep packing it all into your
foundering vessel until it sinks? Consider an impertinent suggestion from
an outsider - approach whatever branch of the Environmental Protection A-
gency is concerned with the resources being wasted and the spaces being
polluted, and have them help you make the "industry" mend its ways. An
EPA-endorsed edict should be possible: "By the year X the percentage of
paper in your effluent (speaking to the publishers) has to be under Percentage A; and by year Y it must be below half that." Really, who is
rightfully in control here? Note that you manage the reservoirs that contain what is going to be increasingly recognized as society's greatest resource, its accumulated knowledge.

The Future Knowledge Forms

It is implicit in my impertinent suggestion that microform is probably what librarians will have to count on for a first major transition.
But my longer-term feeling, based upon my extensive involvement with computerized knowledge systems, is that microform in turn will give way to
the electronic form of computer storage - the form in which most of it will
be generated in the first place, and in which it will be stored, accessed,
communicated, and used. I can see no other course. Really, I don't know
whether to feel more embarrassed because I am telling you something that
is probably also obvious to you, or because I am coming across as a brash,
unrealistic futurist.

The Computer Supporting the Individual Knowledge Worker

At SRI, we have developed a way of working with computer support to
typewriter and display terminals that provides really significant support
to a skilled worker for the minute-by-minute, day-after-day work that he

does - the composing, studying, and modifying of his memoranda, plans, designs, and working notes, the reading and answering of his computer-transmitted mail, and the management of his working records. The functions provided by the computer, and the means for the user to control them, have evolved under constant use for over a decade. Now, for instance, if I go to my office on a Saturday when there are no interruptions, I can put in thirteen hours at a display console and walk away feeling positively buoyant. The speed and flexibility with which I could move through my knowledge base, reorganizing here, sending off a message, composing some substantial memoranda that could evolve and take shape like well-behaved plastic under the control of fabrication tools that are a joy to use. Really, the feeling of being able to do at any minute what one's mind needs to deal with right then is very gratifying.

The point I want to make here is that the computer terminal will become the window into the knowledge worker's virtual workplace. His privately organized personal knowledge base and his familiar and constantly used tools provide him the craftsman's environment for skillfully plying his trade. He will come to be absorbed in that world behind the screen; and it will be quite independent of the world around him. He can reach into his working world from any suitable terminal. And they really will become as portable as a miniature TV now is, and eventually be available in the size of a hand calculator.

The effect of this "environmental" change on libraries? Well, such workers will be very much accustomed to "reaching through" their terminals to access, study and manipulate their working information. They will not only be highly skilled at it, which affects the library system's "user-oriented" design criteria, but also they will have highly seasoned preferences for working this way. Indeed, it isn't the library system that will shape their knowledge-work habits. The technological changes occurring in their daily working environment will in fact dictate to the libraries what sort of working interfaces are best for the people at the input and output interfaces of their library systems.

Prototype of Computer-Supported, Recorded Dialog System

One special application area for which we have developed computer aids, and which would tend to have special implications in the library world, is the collaborative dialog between workers distributed in space and time. It is in fact an activity in which the individual knowledge worker engages extensively - a recorded dialog with himself. His notes and files of today are constructed to carry to the person that is himself at a later date what today's person has to communicate. Among a group of collaborators, the recorded aspect of dialog becomes even more important, and our system provides special support to the two service aspects of retrieval and access.

We have a repository system called the Journal. Computerized memoranda or documents submitted to the Journal are each automatically given an accession number and stored in a manner that guarantees the same kind of "frozen record" as if it were published. The system guarantees that a user can gain on line access to that computer record if he has the access number (unless the author declared it private).

Catalog data for computer-held indices are established at entry time, and can be updated subsequently; they provide a basic retrieval service via on-line terminals, or with computer-generated printed indices.

But perhaps the most effective feature in this system is the access automatically provided from citation *links* (specially formatted reference citations in the computer-held text of any on-line memo or document). An on-line link embedded in a passage of a document, when seen by an on-line user, can be pointed to with a suitable command, and the computer will automatically access not just the referenced document, but the exact passage cited in the link. And because the computer can provide such passage-specific access, workers begin to make their citations to specific passages. For instance, a one-sentence memoranda now is quite powerful, e.g. "Jack, shouldn't you reconsider (24351, 4d) in light of Fred's initial policy statement (21087, 2a)?" The author of this memo didn't have to fill in any extra contextual material, or quote from the cited passage, since he knew that Jack would have easy access to them.

The parallel to a library's services is quite obvious. But this system doesn't have skilled catalogers and reference librarians to enrich the service. It also has neither the quality assurance nor the publication barriers provided by editors. But note that while automation of the system lost these human services, there are some very redeeming features. In the first place, catalogers and editors could be re-introduced, and for selected entries this probably will be done. But more important is that this automation, in bringing the workers' everyday working information into a highly effective recorded-dialog service, will find a much larger (by volume) market for its services than does the recorded-dialog service of today's library system.

Add to this observation a further consideration - that heavy personal use of such computer support will extend into the storage, management, retrieval, and access of all of the individual's personal working information. And again, the individual will spend considerably more time using such tools on his "local" working information than he will on the reference information represented by today's library collections.

So we see that tomorrow's knowledge worker will be highly impacted by automation of his local working environment. And also, that the way he deals with recorded dialog in that environment will tend to set the stage for how he will want to handle cross citations, retrieving, and accessing of information as provided via a library-like service institution.

Several scale factors have been significant in our experiment:

1. Instant publication, providing a much more dynamic dialog.
2. Practicable, very-short documents, also favoring a much more dynamic dialog.
3. Passage-specific citation, enabling a citation to support itself better, leading to tighter inter-linking of concepts and facts, and supporting the brief entries.
4. Instant access, supporting the citation practice, encouraging people to publish (less fear of it being buried, one simple citation to bring it into currency later on). Browsing takes on a new effectiveness.

These quantitative differences from today's library-style recorded-dialog service produce very significant qualitative differences. The power is apparent, the technology is obviously going to provide it at reasonable cost, and the inevitability of widespread use of such techniques seems unarguable. Will the libraries adapt? In time to be relevant?

A Note About Communication Technology

The amazing emergence of the low-cost calculator over the past few years has helped all of us be aware that digital-computer technology really will make cheap and plentiful the availability of computer storage and processing. A related trend in communications will also have significant impact on the library world. Information converted to digital form can be processed and stored with such promising flexibility and low cost (in light of the explosion in digital micro-electronics), that exploration of a new form of communication system over the past six years has opened a promise of extremely cheap and flexible communication. In this "packet communication system," the communication between any two points is parcelled up into modular chunks called *packets* (much as today's container shipping does for cargo transportation). A packet carries its own destination information, and is routed through the communication network by special mini-computers at each node. These computers know about traffic conditions, and pick the best route. Packets carrying document information would zip through the system along with packets containing speech segments, cash-transaction data, weather reports, etc. Very efficient use of satellites and cheap ground stations are expected.

The Advanced Research Projects Agency (ARPA) of the Department of Defense has an experimental computer network (ARPANET) that pioneered this communication principle, and has been conducting advanced research to improve its general applicability. My group has participated in the development and exploratory application of ARPANET. Currently our knowledge-worker support service is delivered via this network to hundreds of users across the country. This experience has produced a very strong appreciation within me for this impact of digital-packet communications on the future of our information systems.

In a world of very cheap digital systems and very cheap digital communications, the pressure will be very intense toward converting knowledge systems from a paper to an electronic base. Workers will anyway be making very heavy use of computer support for doing their everyday knowledge work. They won't think anything of connecting to computers or other workers across the country; they will be perfectly calm about subscribing to computerized library services from great distances. In my laboratory today, a worker would sooner connect through to Cambridge from his terminal to access a given service than he would walk to another office (much less another building) to access the service. There won't be a market for a special terminal that connects to the library. The worker will not only want to be able to switch his terminal to the library's information system, he'll want the information obtained from the library to be in a mode electronically transferrable into his personal, computerized workshop, to integrate into his notes and working information.

One of our uses of ARPANET's communication facility is to have the computer interconnect the display terminals of two distant workers. While they talk on the telephone, they see the same views of their working material, and either party can control the computer to invoke any tool or access any information to use as needed in support of their dialog. This will be a common type of communication in the future. It means that a reference specialist can work with a remote user this way, too, helping him locate and select his material from a large information base that the specialist knows about. Neither the specialist nor the worker must be located near the computer, which in turn needn't be near the information store.

What seems sure to evolve for the knowledge industry is a much more open market place. No longer will a large building, warehousing every docment to which access is important, located physically near to its users, be necessary.

Conclusion

My message today is quite similar to the one I delivered at the ADI meeting in Berkeley, December 1959. Fifteen years' growth in the library burden makes the overwhelm seem more real; fifteen years have transformed the computer and communication technology, and we all can believe that its service will be there if we can harness it; fifteen years of complete absorption by me in pursuing what the technology can offer to increase the knowledge workers' potential therein. When I integrate these perspectives, I reach the same conclusions: the way that the information will be generated in the first place, the way that humans who serve the library institution will be able to work, and the way that the users of the library services will be doing their everyday knowledge work, are going to be affected so heavily by the computer-communication technology that it is the library system that will adapt to them and not vice versa.

One day there will be a turning point reached. How soon I don't know. It won't be when the computer people advise you of it. It will be the day when the decisions that begin the significant transition become in magnitude and impact of a scope that your institutional decision-makers can deal with them within their existing budgets, commitments, knowledge, political adroitness, risk limits, and timing framework. To my mind, it isn't until the technologists provide you with alternatives that meet these conditions that the ball is actually in your court.

Acknowledgment is given to the sponsors of Mr. Englebart's research over the past decade:
   Advanced Research Projects Agency (ARPA)
   Rome Air Development Center (RADC)
   Office of Naval Research (ONR)
   Langley Research Center, NASA

DISCUSSION

Roth (to Englebart): If the energy availability level remains a problem, what happens to the support for the kind of operation you propose?

Englebart: There are a lot of unknown changes. The direct energy consumption by individuals who make heavy use of this system isn't going to be very large in comparison to the secondary effects of its use. For instance, your transportation needs change a little bit, are reduced; and the change in energy consumption due to that factor could easily mask out the new energy this system requires. It's a very interesting thing to consider for environment and energy questions: the amount of travel that needs to be involved in acquiring information can be cut down considerably.

As an experiment, we have had a man working very closely with us as part of our staff, for six years now. He lives a hundred miles away, and he comes in once a week. The rest of the time he's at the end of a terminal. We have a deal, he's paying for that experiment. He wants to live up there by Occidental and we cut his salary by the amount it costs to communicate, and he's happy as a lamb; he's very productive.

There isn't any direct prediction I feel at all safe in making about it, but there'll just be a lot of associated changes. I think, if anything, we have a better chance to cope with the energy problem and the environment problem and the transportation problem.

Question from the audience (to Englebart): It was interesting, of course, to see you manipulate the terminal with things like your past correspondence and citations to articles, but if you apply the problems you brought up before about the scale of things, if you had a library of ten million volumes, is it realistic to assume that you can manipulate information through a terminal when the problems of scale come up?

Englebart: The staging and warehousing and choices about where you aggregate what kinds of materials and the processes are just so immensely more flexible when the information is in this electronic form that avenues of solution are incredibly freer. Whether or not we can cope with it, we have a much better chance than we do now. The individual will have his own work place that's very familiar, and it will be tuned to him with a vocabulary that suits him for controlling this device. Through that you can reach to many kinds of services, including special support people who in turn can be linked by telephone. They in turn can go do things in bigger bases. This great chance, the sorting out of the roles that are supplied by libraries, re-apportionment and that kind of topological configuration is part of the solution that has to come. There will still be needs for people who know their way

around special large data bases to find things for people, and
there will still be a lot of need for human support in that
whole system.

Karl Vollmayer: I am from the Redwood City Public Library, which is 25
miles south of San Francisco, for those of you who are out of
state. I've been most interested in Mr. Englebart's comments.
We feel very honored and privileged in Redwood City, being one of
the four libraries in the Bay Area participating in an experiment
that's now in its second year. It's an experiment headed by the
National Science Foundation. It consists of placing in four public libraries a terminal which connects us to the computer at
Lockheed which goes by the name of DIALOG. I won't presume to
tell you anything about it here because it's much too difficult
for me to do so in detail. The terminal works for us in providing a higher level of service to the public. I see our own oper-
tion of this terminal in an entirely new light after hearing what
Mr. Englebart said. The ability to look at, pull out, relate,
and make enough new associations with all kinds of information
and to do it with great speed is exciting. I would like to tell
you what this does for our collection. We're a small public library of only 150,000 volumes, but the addition of this terminal
in our main library gives us access to five million documents
which we do not own. It provides our public with this tremendously enriched resource and does it with the speed that could not be
equalled even with a whole staff of librarians trying to search
the material manually.

Englebart: I wander up and use your library. I live only a few miles
south, and I come with my eleven-year-old son, and we go after
all sorts of strange things. The two of us together haven't had
nerve enough to try that terminal yet, but I'd really like to, so
if our nerve gets high enough, we will. Can you run the terminal?

Vollmayer: No, but our staff can.

Englebart: Anyway, you can hand me to someone that can hold my hand. I
really freely admit that when you walk up to anybody else's computer, there's a barrier. There are things to learn about it.
It's not unlike going into someone's tool shop. He has everything laid out differently, and it takes time to learn. There
has been a lot of contention in the manned-computer field for
years about how easy to learn the tools should be. People forget
to note that there's a whole spectrum of people that are going to
use it. At one end, there's the vending machine person who wants
to know which handle to pull to buy a comb or something. At the
other end, there is a professional that's going to live in that
environment and work, and you're just a terrible disservice if
you don't allow his vocabulary to grow. He invests years of
learning. Everyone here has invested years of learning the methods and terminology of his work place.

Nolan Lushington (directed to Englebart): I wondered if you had any ex-
        periments or if any thought had been given to utilizing this
        kind of set-up for non-verbal kinds of communication. We've been
        talking about duplicating the printed word, or almost reproducing
        libraries or access to libraries or cross-referencing our commun-
        ications. It's all been very verbal. It seems to me that there
        is a whole area of communications that perhaps a lot of people
        are much more comfortable with than the verbal area that we're
        talking about, and it seems to be that this is such a marvelous
        device to get into that whole other kind of thing. I wondered if
        you could share some of your thoughts or ideas about that.

Englebart: Well, that's what I was referring to when I made a comment to
        say it's still unexplored, all the advantage that potentially is
        there for new forms of portraying your thoughts, new structures
        and forms. If you really have a much improved support tool for
        creating the forms and organizing them and manipulating them, the
        type of symbology we use can extend a lot. The language we hap-
        pen to have settled on and the printed form of it had to be influ-
        enced heavily by the physical means we had to create the external
        symbols. There's a whole virgin area to explore to discover how
        we really symbolize the kind of thoughts we have.

Lushington: I wonder if there have been any actual experiments with com-
        puter access to an array of films or slides or other kinds of non-
        verbal communication. I just wondered if there was anything like
        that in existence.

Englebart: Well, I know that at Xerox Research Center in Palo Alto they're
        playing with displays on which you can paint colors and things on
        them and get all sorts of effects which open the media, but we
        don't know any concerted attempt to just open up and go. I have
        a feeling that the meaningful experiments won't occur until you
        have people who are used to working in these areas and then given
        tools and methods by which other forms of media can be employed.
        Then their vocabulary begins to expand. Incidentally, it won't
        be long until it's practical to encode spoken speech with high
        resolution, compactly in digital form, so that you can send com-
        muniques. Then you can see a reference to a given passage of
        speech that's recorded by this device, and you can point to the
        link, and you'll hear that passage of speech coming back. So
        there are many exciting things coming.

Roth (directed to Propst): Is the service that your agency renders avail-
        able for a fee or is it something done in terms of purchasing e-
        quipment eventually from the Herman Miller Corporation?

Propst: Neither. The projects are research collaborations with institu-
        tions. We join them, we commit funds, efforts, and research
        teams; they commit site, personnel, situations; so this is always
        a collaboration with another organization. We invite investiga-

tions all the time, potential sites to try this, so it's a joint investment. The purpose is not to launch furnishings; it's really to experiment in a realistic way with an environment; these are genuine research projects.

Englebart: There's no way the kind of thing I'm working on is going to get out there and work without services such as Mr. Propst offers, and that's one of the hopes I have that sometime somebody will have enough need and support his seeing what it takes to integrate what we have into an environment that's whole. We can't possibly cover that whole scope.

Propst: I think we would temper Mr. Englebart's projection a little bit, because we still see a more diverse arena than merely the individual and the terminal. We recognize the need for seeing how human relationships work, seeing people, drawing people, directing that population, dealing with an environment full of signals. But we still have to read, we need a place for that.

Englebart: I acknowledge all that very freely. I was describing what could be done and if you're in these areas, the freedom it gives you. It still has to be resolved how you associate when you withdraw from that.

Propst: Carrying the culture forward, carrying society interaction along, too, that is another aspect of life with each other in big organizations. Simply to be in a live society full of all those marvelous things, making it seem an interesting personal place to be - this is the environment we want to support and develop.

Englebart: I've been thinking for many years about the cultural impact and change that has to go along with the integration of exotic new tools. There's no way that you just can slip the new tools into an old culture without having to adapt attitudes, feelings, roles, beliefs, and habits. I'm not saying that this wonderful technology is going to force you to that. What I'm saying is that technology offers some wonderful potentials. You are not going to be able to harness it in harmony with being human without adapting your culture, which anyway is a product of all this mix of physical environment and roles that we've been living in the past. Culture has to keep evolving with the new. Somebody can help facilitate humanly sensible evolution. There's nobody I know like Mr. Propst to help do that, so I'd like to see him tackle institutions and mix them.

McAdams: I can't resist asking Mr. Englebart: When you get in your computer and fly around, you're obviously not going to encounter anything that hasn't been put into the data base, and there's a lot of effort involved in building that data base. With computer networks, you can save a lot of duplication of effort in building larger and larger data bases, but at some point again don't

you reach a point of scale where there's a lot of deadwood in
there, as much deadwood as we have in our libraries?

Englebart: Yes, but I don't have to wade through it. The way you can ar-
rrange your access support, you can just say, "Well, I only want
to see those items by a certain author, those since a certain
date" without much trouble and soon your own collections emerge
and the stuff that to you is inconsequential just drifts down out
of your sight. There's certainly ecological problems in all that.
There's a lot to learn about it.
    One thing Mr. Propst raised yesterday which I have thought a-
bout off and on through the years but few others have is that if
you're working in an environment like that, you are accessible to
messages and linking and close communication to so many other people that you could just literally get drowned. That's true. If
this is successfully integrated there have to be some new kinds
of cultural modes and agreements in working out how you limit the
people to whom you will agree to have access. You have to test
and see if you can make acceptable the evolution to harness these
things. I'm not blind at all. I get excited by the potential and
try to stay sober about the problems that undoubtedly will be associated with it.

Craig Moore: I'm fairly new in the library game, and engineering-mathema-
tician-systems-type thinking is the kind of thinking that I'm
accustomed to, so what Mr. Englebart says is right up my line.
For those who are, I think probably few of us have not been introduced to this kind of thinking. For a recent and, I think, interesting and adequate survey article on this, the last issue of
Business Week has a rather good spread on this whole idea of word
processing. However, I think we do have to bring ourselves back
to earth. I've been working both with librarians and administrators and with faculty members at the University of Missouri, and
I've heard a remark about how the technology is changing with regard to information and libraries. The quest for other media for
information storage has been discussed for decades and still we
are laboring along under the weight of the printed word, and I
think several of our speakers have said we will continue to do so
for several years. Mr. Englebart agrees that this technology is
still some years away, so I think we still face the questions,
"How can we cope now? How much of, how long should, our plans be
reaching into the future to cope with the printed word and when
can we stop worrying about the space problem and just worry about
accommodating a group of new terminals?" Classics professors, for
example, at the University of Missouri will never accept the fact
that they can work through this kind of technological means.
They must lay their hands on these ancient books and see these ancient coins, and they must sit in crypts. They prefer the darkly
lit stacks, and this is where true research goes on. I think we
have to cope with not only the very newest way of thinking but

with the very oldest. We're still stuck in the corner. What
should we do right now? I think this is healthy thinking, but
I haven't reached any resolutions myself.

Conclusion

The purpose of the preconference was to provide a framework for librarians and other participants to explore the various alternatives to resolve library space problems and to discuss the implications of these alternatives for space, cost, public service, and staff. The proceedings reveal that there is no single, absolute answer for these problems. The answer for each library will be found in a unique combination of components derived from a variety of alternatives. This requires a fresh and creative approach to the problem which must be faced now. It cannot be put aside for the future, or it will be subject to the haphazard pressures of circumstance, and the solution will no longer lie within the library's prerogative.

The papers presented were limited in scope in that the speakers described what decisions were made at a particular institution at a particular time, or they described the state of technology for a specific alternative. Decisions are profoundly influenced by the institutional or societal pressures present, or absent, whether they are generated by the budget, the site, energy considerations, the faculty, the public, technology, or some other current dilemma or trend. The result is that these proceedings are not exhaustive in coverage of any alternative nor will they necessarily provide *the* answer to any one library's quandary.

The preconference illustrated clearly that history repeats itself. Problems prevalent at the beginning of this century are again prevalent in the 1970s; solutions considered at the turn of the century, or variations thereof, are still being considered as viable alternatives to the library space problem. Technology has made some impact on these alternatives, but not as substantial as one might have expected from an era of splitting the atom and space exploration. The costs are still prohibitive for wholesale acceptance of some of the technologically advanced alternatives. Librarians resist adopting technical developments in which they detect the potential to seriously erode the quality of their service to the public. It may be a mature twenty-first century before there is significant acceptance of technologies which can save space; but, perhaps, by that time the library will be a substantially different kind of institution.